The Vitamin and Health Encyclopedia

REVISED

The Vitamin and Health Encyclopedia

REVISED

By Jack Ritchason, N.D., Ph. D.

Published by
Woodland Books
P.O. Box 1422
Provo, Utah 84603

ISBN 0-913923-52-4

While every effort is made to guarantee the timeliness and authenticity of all information researched and presented in this publication, the ever-changing nature of the many activities underlying the facts, figures, trends, and theories presented makes impossible unqualified reliance on the material herein. Further, nothing herein is to be construed as a substitute for consultation with a qualified expert. Reasonable caution is the watchword of good heatlh.

Printed in the United States of America

Table of Contents

ABOUT THE AUTHOR

Dr. Jack Ritchason has been in the health field since 1963. He is a much-in-demand lecturer on herbs, vitamins, nutrition and Iridology and has lectured both nationally and internationally.

Dr. Ritchason graduated as a naturopathic doctor from Arizona College of Naturopathic Medicine, a branch of the American University of Natural Therapeutics and Preventative Medicine. He has his Ph.D. in Nutrition from Donsbach University and has done graduate work in homeopathy in Missouri and also a F.I.T. in Florida.

Dr. Ritchason is a charter board member of Iridologists International. He is a member of the State Society of Homeopathic Physicians, is a master herbalist and the dean of the Herbal Intstitute in Huntington Beach, California.

Dr. Ritchason is a Life Member of the National Health Federation (NHF) and is on the board of Governors of the NHF. He is a registered healthologist and is a certified instructor for Touch for Health. He is also considered to be one of the top Iridologists and teachers of Iridology today.

Dr. Ritchason is the author of the book *The Little Herb Encyclopedia Revised,* one of the top selling herbal books today. It is published in both English and Spanish.

ACKNOWLEDGMENT

I would like to acknowledge the expert help which my secretary, Karen Krein, has given in the completion of this book.

I would also like to thank my wife, Verlyn, for her help and support in working on this book.

Jack Ritchason

Dr. Ritchason's
TEN GOLDEN RULES OF
HEALTH

1. Stop putting poisons into the body.

2. It takes 5-7 times the normal amount of nutrition to build and repair than it does to maintain.

3. Nothing heals in the human body in less than 3 months, then add one month for every year that you have been sick.

4. Have moderation in all things.

5. Make peace with nature.

6. Live closer to God.

7. You must take responsibility for yourself and your health.

8. Eat as much raw food as possible.

9. Exercise regularly the rest of your life.

10. Practice and learn to understand completely Hering's law of cure, which is "All cure starts from within out and from the head down and in reverse order as the symptoms have appeared."

Introduction

Life was intended to be rich and rewarding. Man was created and placed on earth to experience the full spectrum of life's opportunities. We have the capacity to know and enjoy the beauties of the natural world, the warmth of good interpersonal relationships, the fulfillment of achieving our goals. But central to our ability to enjoy life is the necessity of maintaining good health. The Apostle Paul understood this principle and it was written in John: '...I wish above all things that thou mayest prosper and *be in health...*" (3John:2).

All the Old Testament prophets were commanded to fast and to care for their bodies by making use of those natural foods available to them. Christ himself referred to his body as a temple (see John 2:21) and followed the pattern of fasting and using wholesome foods to maintain that temple.

The same principles are true for modern man: WE MUST SUSTAIN OURSELVES PHYSICALLY IN ORDER TO BE AT OUR BEST INTELLECTUALLY, SPIRITUALLY, AND EMOTIONALLY. The earth's abundance can still give us that sustenance, but our lives are now so complicated that we rarely can rely on diet alone to provide all the nutrients and chemicals our bodies require to function. Such commonplace and apparently harmless elements of daily living as refined sugars, white flour, city sunlight, daily stresses, cocktails, and aspirin actually rob us of the nutrients we need to live! It is no wonder that vitamin and mineral supplements are so vital to our health: they restore the natural substances our bodies use up in keeping us going.

1

About This Book

The Vitamin and Health Encyclopedia puts the information you need about supplements right into your hands. You don't need to wade through pages of meaningless detail to find what you want. It includes alphabetical listings of conditions which respond to vitamin and mineral treatment and of the characteristics and uses of individual vitamins and minerals as well.

The information is basic, helpful, and easy to find. The first section lists many common conditions which may be treated with vitamins and minerals. Several suggestions are made for each condition: you may find that one vitamin or one combination works better than another for you.

The second and third sections catalogue the vitamins and minerals themselves in alphabetical order, giving a little information about each one, listing the benefits of its use, and suggesting its best natural sources. It is intended that you may use these sections as a cross-reference with the first if you wish. In the paragraphs explaining benefits you will find key words in italics to draw your attention immediately to the ailments or conditions concerned. This makes it easier and faster for you to find a complete list of optional answers to your particular question.

For example, a quick glance at Section One will tell you vitamins C, K, and P might be helpful if you bruise easily. If you are interested in exactly how vitamin C affects bruises, simply look up vitamin C in Section Two and scan the page quickly until the word *bruises* catches your eye. Then you can immediately read exactly what you want to know about vitamin C without spending time looking through its other uses. The fourth section gives you information on the Bach Flower Remedies (which are for the emotions in the body) which are actually low potency homeopathic remedies for such. Section five will fill you in on the building blocks of life. These are called Amino Acids. The body must have the proper abundance and the proper combinations at all times in order for the body to be healthy. Section six tells us of the Raw Glandulars. We can go back to Hippocrates, the father of mdeicine, who taught us the basis of using the heart for heart, liver for liver, and brain for brain, again following the principle of "like cures like."

Preface

Vitamins and minerals generally work to support and encourage the body's natural functions. Deficiencies of vitamins and minerals can cause those functions to slow down, to occur inappropriately, or to fail. For this reason, deficiencies must be corrected.

Even those whose diets would supply all the vitamins and minerals they could normally use may have deficiencies for one reason or another. Stress at work, air pollution, pain, illness, even use of prescription drugs to combat disease can deplete vitamin and mineral supplies to deficiency levels. For this reason, regular supplements and a ready reference to symptoms and specific aids for problems as they arise can be your strongest ally in restoring and maintaining your health.

The beauty of vitamin and mineral treatment is that it is totally natural: it uses substances your body needs, substances your system was designed to use. Unlike treatment with drugs, vitamins and minerals add no foreign chemicals to the body, and they produce no side effects. They do not take control of the body; rather, they maintain an environment in which the body regains and sustains control of itself.

Of course, this does not mean that vitamin and mineral supplements can ward off or quickly cure serious illnesses. Vitamins and minerals help the body correct health problems. They do not correct inherited or chronic disorders or reverse the effects of critical health problems. The body is the master; vitamins and minerals are the tools and materials for the body to rebuild itself.

VITAMINS AND MINERALS DURING PREGNANCY

The old saying "You're eating for two now" is pretty widely acknowledged as false. While a pregnant woman does *not* eat for two, her body does supply nutrients to her unborn child, providing it with the material to develop normally. The expectant mother's energy requirements may increase as much as 300 calories per day; a nursing mother can expend an extra 1,000 calories a day. Obviously, these are conditions under which the health of both mother and baby are dependent upon the mother's understanding of her increased need for nutrients. The pregnant or nursing woman should supply herself a good multiple vitamin and mineral supplement and be particularly aware of getting enough vitamins B, E, C, and D and sufficient calcium and iron.

CHILDREN

Since vitamins and minerals effect the chemical reaction that changes food into useable proteins, carbohydrates and fats to build tissue and to supply energy, growing children need extra vitamins and minerals. They particularly require calcium and iron and B complex and C vitamins. Because kids expend so much energy and because they tend to supplement their diets themselves with sweets and junk foods, most of them get substantially fewer vitamins and minerals than they really need.

NOT PRESCRIPTIONS

The Vitamin and Health Encyclopedia does not directly or indirectly dispense medical advice or prescribe the use of vitamins and minerals as a form of treatment for sickness without medical approval. It is not the intent of this book to diagnose or prescribe. The information is a collection of various uses of vitamins and minerals from a variety of sources. Only the most common or most widely accepted uses are mentioned. If you decide to diagnose for yourself and use the information without your doctor's approval, you will be prescribing for yourself, which is your constitutional right, but the publisher assumes no responsibility.

Ailments

ACNE

vitamin A, vitamin B2, vitamin B3, B complex, vitamin E, vitamin F, potassium, sulfur

ADRENAL GLAND

vitamin B5, B complex, vitamin C

AGING

vitamin A, vitamin B13, vitamin B15, B complex, vitamin C, vitamin E, calcium, selenium, potassium, sodium

ALZHEIMER'S DISEASE

Lecithin, vitamin E, vitamin C, B Complex. (Refer to Appendix, page 119)

ALCOHOLISM

B complex, particularly vitamin B1; vitamin B15; folic acid; choline; potassium; zinc

ALLERGIES

B complex, particularly vitamin B5; vitamin C; vitamin F; vitamin H; manganese; potassium, vitamin A

AMNESIA

vitamin B6, vitamin B15, B Complex, vitamin B-5

ANEMIA

B complex, particularly vitamin B1, vitamin B6, and vitamin B12; folic acid; vitamin C; vitamin E; vitamin T; cobalt; copper; iron; molybdenum

ANGINA

vitamin B15, B complex, vitamin E, vitamin B - 3

APPETITE

vitamin B1, vitamin B3, vitamin B12, B complex, folic acid, vitamin C, vitamin H, zinc

ARTERIOSCLEROSIS

vitamin A, vitamin B3, B complex, choline, vitamin D, vitamin E, chromium, zinc, cystine

ARTHRITIS

B complex, particularly vitamin B5; vitamin C; vitamin E; vitamin F; calcium; phosphorus; sulfur

ASTHMA

vitamin B12, vitamin B15, B complex, vitamin E

ATHEROSCLEROSIS

vitamin B6, vitamin B15, B complex, folic acid, choline, inositol, vitamin F, vitamin H, iodine, zinc

BAD BREATH

vitamin B3, vitamin B6, B complex

BALDNESS

B complex, particularly vitamin B3, vitamin B5, vitamin B6, folic acid, and inositol; vitamin F; vitamin H; PABA; copper

BEE STINGS

vitamin B1, B complex, as repellant

BERIBERI

vitamin B1, B complex

BIRTH DEFECTS

Protein, B complex, vitamin E, vitamin B2 deficiency in mother may cause birth defects

BLINDNESS

B complex, vitamin A, vitamin B2 (twilight blindness), vitamin C

BLOOD

to build-B complex, vitamin B5, vitamin B6, folic acid, vitamin B12, vitamin C, vitamin D, cobalt, iron; to encourage clotting-vitamin K; to encourage coagulation-vitamin T; to dissolve blood clots-vitamin E

BLOOD PRESSURE

to regulate-choline; to reduce high blood pressure-vitamin B3, vitamin B6, vitamin B15, B complex, vitamin E, chromium, potassium

BOILS

vitamin A, vitamin C

BONES

vitamin A, vitamin C, vitamin D, calcium, fluorine, manganese, phosphorus

BONES (FRACTURED)

vitamin A, vitamin C, vitamin E, calcium

BRAIN

inositol, potassium, sulfur, zinc, lecithin

BRONCHITIS

vitamin A, vitamin C, vitamin E

BRUISES

vitamin C, vitamin K, vitamin P, calcium, Bach Flower Remedy #39

BURNS

B complex, vitamin C, vitamin E, PABA, zinc, Bach Flower Remedy #39

CANCER

vitamin B12, vitamin B17, B complex, vitalin C, selenium

CANDIDA ALBICANS

Glandulars such as Thymus, vitamin A, vitamin C, Acidophilus, B Complex (from a yeast-free source). (See Candida Albicans in the Appendix, page 120)
vitamin B3, B complex, Lysine

CANKER SORES

vitamin B3, B complex, folic acid, candida albicans

CARBUNCLES

vitamin A, vitamin C, Cataracts, B complex, calcium, B2

CHICKEN POX

vitamin C, vitamin E, vitamin A

CHOLESTEROL

vitamin B3, vitamin B6, vitamin B15, B complex, choline, vitamin F, inositol, vitamin C, lecithin, vanadium, zinc, selenium

CIRCULATORY SYSTEM

vitamin B3, vitamin B15, B complex, vitamin E, calcium, magnesium, niacin, oral chelation

COLDS

vitamin A, vitamin C, vitamin D, vitamin P, water

COLD SORES

vitamin A, vitamin C, vitamin E, B complex

COLITIS

vitamin B6, B complex, vitamin E, vitamin K, calcium, iron, potassium

CONSTIPATION

choline, vitamin C, vitamin E, calcium, water, potassium, magnesium, acidophilus

CONVULSIONS

vitamin B6, B complex, calcium, Bach Flower Remedy #39

CUTS

vitamin B5, B complex, vitamin C, vitamin E, calcium, vitamin A

DANDRUFF

selenium, B complex

DEPRESSION

vitamin B12, B complex, vitamin H, magnesium, calcium, flower essence

DIABETES

B complex, vitamin E, chromium, manganese, potassium, zinc, silica

DIARRHEA

vitamin B1, vitamin B3, B complex, folic acid, calcium

DIGESTION

for digestive problems - vitamin B3, inositol, chlorine, magnesium, manganese; for converting foods into energy vitamin B1, vitamin B2, vitamin B5, vitamin B6, vitamin B12, B complex, folic acid, sodium, zinc, HCL-pepsin, enzymes

DIZZINESS

vitamin B6, vitamin B15, vitamin B3, B complex, vitamin E, choline, vitamin P, iron

DRY SKIN

vitamin A, vitamin D, vitamin E, vitamin F

EAR INFECTIONS

vitamin A, vitamin B6, B complex, vitamin C, vitamin P

ECZEMA

vitamin A, B complex, inositol, vitamin F, vitamin H, PABA, silica

EMPHYSEMA

vitamin A, vitamin B15, Vitamin B3, B complex, vitamin C, vitamin E, calcium

EXHAUSTION

vitamin B5, vitamin B12, vitamin B15, B complex, folic acid, vitamin C, vitamin D, vitamin E, vitamin H, iron, manganese, zinc

EYE DISORDERS

vitamin A, vitamin B2, vitamin B12, B complex, vitamin C, inositol, vitamin D, vitamin E, calcium

FATIGUE

vitamin B5, vitamin B15, B complex, vitamin C, vitamin E, vitamin H, iron, manganese, potassium

FOOT PROBLEMS

for discomfort-vitamin B1; for cold feet-take iodine, vitamin B3; for athlete's foot-B complex, apply vitamin C powder

FEVER

vitamin A, vitamin B1, B complex, vitamin C, sodium, water, enema

FOOD POISONING

folic acid, vitamin A, vitamin C

GANGRENE

vitamin B15, B complex, vitamin C, vitamin E, vitamin A

GASTROINTESTINAL SYSTEM

vitamin A, vitamin B3, B complex, vitamin B6

GALLSTONES

vitamin A, vitamin B6, B complex, vitamin E, magnesium, vitamin C

GENITOURINARY SYSTEM

vitamin A, B complex, vitamin C, vitamin E

GLANDS

vitamin A, vitamin C, B complex

GOITER

iodine

GROWTH

vitamin B1, vitamin B2, vitamin B12, B complex, chromium, iodine, iron, phosphorus, zinc, vitamin C, vitamin E, calcium, protein

GUMS

vitamin A, vitamin C, vitamin P, phosphorus

HAIR

vitamin A, vitamin B2, vitamin B6, B complex, folic acid, inositol, vitamin F, vitamin H, PABA, chlorine, iodine, sulfur, protein

HANDS

for numbness-vitamin B6; for cold hands-vitamin B3, vitamin B15, B complex, vitamin E, iodine, iron

HANGOVERS

vitamin B1, vitamin B15, B complex, vitamin C, calcium

HAY FEVER

B complex, pantothenic acid, vitamin C, potassium, vitamin A

HEADACHE

B complex, particularly vitamin B3, vitamin B15, and choline; calcium and magnesium (ratio 2 to 1), vitamin C

HEART

vitamin B1, vitamin B15, B complex, inositol, choline, vitamin D, vitamin E, vitamin F, vitamin K, calcium, magnesium, phosphorus, potassium, vanadium, selenium

HEMOPHILIA

vitamin T, vitamin K, vitamin C

HEMORRHOIDS

vitamin C, vitamin P, vitamin E, calcium, lecithin

HERPES

vitamin A, vitamin B1, B complex, vitamin C, lysine

HIGH BLOOD PRESSURE

calcium, potassium, B complex

HYPERTHYROIDISM

vitamin A, vitamin B1, B complex, vitamin E, PABA, calcium, iodine

HYPOGLYCEMIA

vitamin B5, B complex, vitamin C, vitamin E, calcium, potassium

HYPOTHYROIDISM

iodine, B complex

IMPETIGO

vitamin A, vitamin C, vitamin E, iodine

INFECTIONS (RESISTING AND SPEEDING RECOVERY FROM)

vitamin A, vitamin B5, vitamin B15, B complex, vitamin C, vitamin P, iron, sulfur, water

INFERTILITY

vitamin E, zinc, selenium

INSOMNIA

vitamin B6, vitamin B15, B complex, folic acid, choline, calcium, iron, L-tryptophan, vitamin B3

INTERNAL BLEEDING

vitamin C, vitamin K

INTESTINES, LARGE

acidophilus, vitamin B6, vitamin E, calcium, magnesium

INTESTINES, SMALL

folic acid, inositol

IRRITABILITY

vitamin B12, B complex, calcium, manganese

JOINTS

vitamin C, sulfur, calcium, sodium, silica

KIDNEYS

vitamin B6, B complex, choline, vitamin C, phosphorus

KIDNEY STONES

vitamin B6, B complex, magnesium, vitamin C

LACTATION

vitamin B1, vitamin B2, B complex, folic acid, vitamin D, calcium, vitamin A

LEG (CRAMPS)

vitamin B1, vitamin B3, vitamin B6, vitamin B15, B complex, vitamin E, vitamin H, calcium, magnesium

LIPS

vitamin B2, B complex

LIVER

vitamin A, vitamin B1, vitamin B6, vitamin B13, vitamin B15, B complex, insositol, choline, vitamin K, sulfur, lecithin

LUNGS

vitamin A, vitamin E, vitamin C, potassium

MEASLES

vitamin A, vitamin C, vitamin E

MENOPAUSE

B complex, vitamin E, calcium, selenium

MENSTRUATION

B complex, particularly vitamin B6; vitamin K; vitamin E; calcium; iron; zinc

MENTAL ATTITUDE

vitamin B1, B complex, iodine

MENTAL CAPACITIES

vitamin B12, B complex, choline, iodine, lecithin, manganese, potassium, zinc

MENTAL DISORIENTATION

vitamin B3, vitamin B15, B complex, calcium, flower essence

MENTAL ILLNESS

vitamin B3, vitamin B12, vitamin B15, folic acid, vitamin H, calcium, magnesium, flower essence

19

MENTAL RETARDATION

vitamin B6, vitamin B15, B complex, vitamin D, vitamin E, iodine

METABOLISM

vitamin B1, vitamin B2, vitamin B5, vitamin B6, vitamin B12, B complex, folic acid, vitamin D, vitamin H, manganese, sodium

MIGRAINE HEADACHES

B complex, particularly vitamin B3, calcium, panothetic acid, vitamin E, vitamin C

MISCARRIAGE (PREVENTION)

vitamin C, vitamin E, vitamin P, B complex

MONONUCLEOSIS

vitamin A, B complex, large doses of vitamin C, potassium

MORNING SICKNESS

vitamin B1, vitamin B6, B complex, vitamin K

MOTION SICKNESS

vitamin B1, vitamin B6, B complex

MOUTH

vitamin B2, vitamin B3, vitamin B5, vitamin B6, B complex

MUCOUS MEMBRANES

vitamin A, vitamin B2, B complex, vitamin C

MULTIPLE SCLEROSIS AND ALS

vitamin B12, vitamin B13, B complex, lecithin, vitamin E, calcium and magnesium, HCL, minerals (See Appendix for more detail, page 124)

MUSCLES

vitamin B1, vitamin B6, B complex, choline, vitamin C, vitamin E, vitamin H, calcium, magnesium, manganese, sodium, potassium

MUSCULAR DYSTROPHY

inositol, vitamin E, B complex, calcium

NAILS

vitamin A, vitamin B2, B complex, iodine, sulfur, zinc, silica

NEPHRITIS

vitamin B6, B complex, vitamin C, vitamin E

NERVOUS SYSTEM

vitamin A, vitamin B1, vitamin B3, vitamin B6, vitamin B12, B complex, choline, vitamin E, calcium, magnesium, manganese, sodium, lecithin, flower essense

NEURITIS

vitamin B1, B complex, calcium and magnesium

NIGHT BLINDNESS

vitamin A

NOSEBLEEDS

vitamin C, vitamin K, calcium

NURSING

vitamin B1, vitamin B2, B complex, folic acid, vitamin D
calcium

OSTEOMALACIA

vitamin D, calcium

OVERWEIGHT

B complex, particularly vitamin B6; inositol, choline; vitamin F; calcium; iodine; magnesium; phenylalanine

PALSY

vitamin B6, B complex, vitamin E

PAIN

vitamin B1, B complex; folic acid; vitamin K; calcium; vitamin C for back, neck, and leg pain due to injury or spinal disc, Bach Flower Remedy #39

PELLAGRA

vitamin B3, vitamin B6

PHLEBITIS

vitamin C, vitamin E, lecithin

POISON IVY

vitamin A, vitamin C, vitamin E

PREMENSTRUAL SYNDROME (PMS)

vitamin E (800 to 1,200 i.u.'s per day), vitamin C (3,000 to 6,000 mgs. per day), pituitary and thyroid glandulars, iodine, B complex, Pantothenic Acid. (See Premenstrual Syndrome in the Appendix, page 126. Also refer to Candida Albicans)

PROSTATE DISORDERS

vitamin E, vitamin F, zinc, selenium

PSORIASIS

vitamin A, inositol, vitamin C, vitamin E

REPRODUCTIVE SYSTEM

vitamin A, vitamin B2, B complex, vitamin E, manganese, zinc

RESPIRATORY SYSTEM

vitamin A, vitamin E, vitamin C

RESTLESSNESS

vitamin B3, vitamin B6, B complex, calcium

RHEUMATIC FEVER

vitamin A, B complex, vitamin C, vitamin E, vitamin P, PABA

RHEUMATISM

vitamin B15, B complex, vitamin F, vitamin P, calcium, sodium

RICKETS

vitamin D, calcium, phosphorus

SCURVY

vitamin A, vitamin B1, vitamin B3, B complex, vitamin C

SHINGLES

vitamin B12, B complex, calcium, lysine,
Bach Flower Remedy # 39

SHOCK

vitamin B5, B complex, vitamin C, Bach Flower Remedy #39

SINUSITIS

vitamin A, vitamin B5, B complex, vitamin C, vitamin E

SKIN

vitamin A, vitamin B2, vitamin B3, vitamin B6, B complex, vitamin D, vitamin E, folic acid, vitamin F, vitamin H, PABA, iodine, iron, sulfur, silica

SKIN DISORDERS

vitamin A, vitamin B3, vitamin B5, vitamin B6, vitamin B12, B complex, vitamin D, inositol, vitamin E, vitamin F, vitamin H, PABA, sulfur (in creams), silica

SNAKEBITE

vitamin A, vitamin C, vitamin K

SORES

vitamin A, vitamin B2, vitamin B3, B complex, vitamin C, vitamin E, folic acid, zinc

SORE THROAT

vitamin A, vitamin B2, vitamin C, iodine

SPINAL DISC

vitamin C, calcium, sulfur

STRESS (Mental and Physical)

B complex, particularly vitamin B2, vitamin B5, vitamin B6, vitamin B15, folic acid, vitamin C, vitamin E, PABA, magnesium, phosphorus, calcium, Bach Flower Remedy #39

STROKE

B complex, vitamin B6 - large doses, vitamin C, calcium, magnesium

SUNBURN

B complex, vitamin C, PABA

SUNSTROKE

B complex, vitamin C, sodium

TASTE

zinc

TEETH

vitamin A, vitamin B3, vitamin B5, vitamin B6, B complex, vitamin C, vitamin D, calcium, chlorine, fluorine, iodine, magnesium, phosphorus

THROMBOSIS

vitamin E

TONGUE

vitamin B2, vitamin B3, B complex

ULCERS

vitamin A, B complex, folic acid, vitamin C, vitamin E, vitamin P, vitamin U, calcium

VARICOSE VEINS

vitamin C, vitamin E, calcium

VENEREAL DISEASE

vitamin A, vitamin C, and vitamin K to replenish after antibiotics

VISION

vitamin A, vitamin B2, vitamin B3, B complex, vitamin C, vitamin E

WARTS

vitamin A, vitamin E, silica

WEAKNESS

vitamin B1, vitamin B6, B complex, vitamin C, vitamin E, potassium

WEIGHT LOSS

vitamin B1, vitamin B6, B complex, phenylalanine

WOUNDS

vitamin A, vitamin B5, B complex, vitamin C, vitamin E, zinc

Vitamins

Vitamins are organic substances necessary for life. We have to ingest vitamins in or with our food. As a matter of fact, the body connot use vitamins without minerals.

The food we eat is composed of proteins, carbohydrates, and fats which the body converts into energy in a form it can use. In order to do that, the body must have the proper amounts and kinds of vitamins. Balanced vitamins act like a catalyst for use of other nutrients: they are not them selves used, but they start and maintain the chemical reaction through which you burn calories and use up the fuel that feeds your body.

Most vitamins are water soluble. That is, they combine with water in the body to do their job, and then they are carried off and excreted in the urine. Most vitamins remain in your system for two-to-three hours at the longest before they are eliminated. In order to assure day-long vitamin levels, water-soluble vitamins must be taken regularly—either by eating a proper diet or by taking supplemental vitamins such as found in tablet or capsule form. The oil-soluble vitamins - A, D, and E - need for FAT assimilation. If for some reason your diet does not include sufficient fat, the oil-soluble vitamins are available in "dry" or water-soluble form.

In any case, vitamins should be taken before - not between and not in place of - meals. Ideally, they should be taken with breakfast, with lunch, and with dinner, but if your schedule allows you only one time a day for vitamins, make that time with breakfast and try to use time release vitamins. Feed your body every five hours for maximum efficiency.

Try to balance your vitamins to work together. The B

complex, for example, is a group of twenty-two similar vitamins. Even though they are all distinct, none of them work as well alone as the entire group does together. They are never found singly in nature; they are always all there. Other vitamins have partners as well; it is a good idea to combine them for effectiveness.

Vitamin A functions best with - B complex, vitamin D, vitamin E, calcium, phosphorus, and zinc.

Vitamin D functions best with - vitamin A, vitamin C, choline, calcium, and phosphorus.

Vitamin E function best with - B complex, inositol, vitamin C, manganese and selenium.

Vitamin C (ascorbic acid) functions best with bioflavonoids, calcium, and magnesium.

Folic acid (folacin) functions best with - B complex and vitamil C.

Niacin functions best with - vitamin B1, vitamin B2, B complex and vitamin C.

Vitamin B1 (thiamine) functions best with - B complex, B2, folic acid, niacin, vitamin C, and vitamin E.

Vitamin B2 (riboflavin) functions best with - vitamin B6, B complex, vitamin C, and niacin.

Vitamin B6 (pyridoxine) functions best with - vitamin B1, vitamin B2, B complex, pantothenic acid, vitamin C, and magnesium.

Vitamin B12 (cyanocobalamin) functions best with vitamin B6, B complex, vitamin C, folic acid, choline, inositol, and potassium.

Calcium functions best with - vitamin A, vitamin C, vitamin D, iron, magnesium, and phosphorus.

Phosphorus functions best with - calcium, vitamin A, vitamin D, iron, and manganese.

Iron functions best with - vitamin B12, folic acid, vitamin C, and calcium.

Magnesium functions best with - vitamin B6, vitamin C, vitamin D, calcium, and phosphorus.

Zinc functions best with - vitamin A, calcium, and phosphorus.

A few vitamins may have toxic effects if taken in massive doses over a long period of time. Watch massive intake of vitamins A and D; avoid combining vitamin A with mineral oil or vitamin E with inorganic iron. It is typically synthetic vitamins which cause reactions. Natural vitamins, even in high doses, are reasonably safe if used wisely.

VITAMIN A

Because vitamin A is fat soluble, it requires fats as well as minerals for proper absorption in the digestive tract.

The body can store vitamin A. As a matter of fact, very large daily doses of vitamin A over a period of months can produce toxic effects. The average dosage of vitamin A is 25,000 to 100,000 units depending on body stresses.

How much "A" is too much? According to Dr. Ray Yancey, research has showed the following:

"*University of Pennsylvania, School of Medicine and The Simon Greenberg Foundation* states: 'We constantly receive inquiries regarding Vitamin A--whether or not it is toxic...40,000 I.U...is the same amount of Vitamin A you would receive if you ate a three ounce portion of calves liver in a restaurant.' Pretty dangerous, huh? But maybe that analogy isn't scientific enough for you--so try these on for size.

University of Pennsylvania, School of Medicine, Department of Dermatology: 'In the treatment of acne vulgaris, the use of Vitamin A was highly efficacious in doses of 300,000 units for women and 400,000 to 500,000 units for men. The danger of hypervitaminosis A in this dosage range has been exaggerated. Vitamin A is a valuable drug for treating stubborn, severely inflammatory acne vulgaris.'

Vitamins--*Ostwald & Briggs:* 'The review of Nieman and Obnbink indicates that, for adults, 1 million I.U. is a toxic dose. Chronic toxic dose for children 1 to 3 years of age was calculated to be about 100,000 I.U. per day with a six month period required before toxicity occurs. It has been reported that cortisone decreases the tolerance to Vitamin A and moderate amounts of Vitamin E or K renders excess amounts of Vitamin A harmless.'

International Journal of Vitamin and Nutrition Research: 'It was determined that a three and one-half year intake of 375,000 I.U. per day for a 150 lb. adult is necessary before any symptoms of Vitamin A toxicity appear.' "

Benefits

In general, vitamin A serves to maintain the body's thin coverings and also its mucous membranes in various organs, systems, and glands. Specifically, vitamin A:

- counteracts *night blindness* and helps heal various disorders of the *eyes* and *vision*

- helps treat such *skin problems* as acne, impetigo, psoriasis, boils, carbuncles, and open ulcers when applied directly

- builds resistance to *colds* and to *infections*, particularly in the *gastrointestinal, urinary,* and *respiratory* systems

- promotes healing of *broken bones* and *damaged skin or organs*

- maintains healthy functioning of the *liver* and *reproductive organs*

- aids in treatment of *emphysema* and *hyperthyroidism*

- promotes *growth* and *maintenance* of healthy *bones, skin, hair, teeth and gums*

- maintains *balance* of *sex hormones*

- shortens the duration of *diseases*

- *cancer*

Natural sources

Green and yellow vegetables, eggs, milk and dairy products, margarine, yellow fruits, liver, fish liver oil, lemon grass.

ACIDOPHILUS

Acidophilus is a friendly bacteria in the bowel. The flora in the bowel can determine the state of health in an individual.

Acidophilus protects your colon from cancer. It is normally established at birth. You need proper amounts of Acidophilus in order to aid digestion and assimilation of foods. The first Acidophilus introduced in a baby is through the colostrum from the mother's milk.

Acidophilus protects us from E. Coli, which causes cancer to form in the colon. Acidophilus is lost through the taking of antibiotics, *excessive* flushing of the colon through enemas or colonics; excessive intake of red meats which have antibiotics in them; coffee also destroys it. Antihistamines, penicillin, and sulpha drugs all destroy the friendly bacteria in the bowel.

Birth control pills also destroy acidophilus. Putrification is **CAUSED** by unfriendly bacteria and acid foods prevent putrification for many of the unfriendly bacteria cannot live in an acid medium. The acidophilus bacillus has the power of fixing itself to the wall of the stomach and exerting its good influence on the contents of the stomach. What this means is the intestines are kept free for longer periods of time from harmful bacteria.

Such people as Ilya Metchnikoff, professor at the Pasteur Institute in Paris, has advanced the theory that unfriendly microbes in the intestine may be responsible for premature death and disease. He believes that the intake of acidophilus can give us a long and healthy life. He says the main therapeutical effect of acidophilus lies in its ability to reduce putrification.

It needs to be stressed that taking acidophilus will in no way harm the effectivness of antibiotics. Anyone taking any kind of antibiotic for any length of time should supplement his diet with acidophilus.

To finalize, Metchnikoff felt that a man consuming acidophilus every day of his life should be able to live to 150 years of age.

Disease will use up the friendly flora also. The bowel should be acid and Acidophilus provides this. The ratio of bacteria in the bowel should be at least 80% Acidophilus to 20% of the unfriendly bacteria. This has been found to be reversed in unhealthy people.

VITAMIN B1 (THIAMINE)

Vitamin B1 is necessary for the body to make full use of its carbohydrate intake.

Sometimes called the "morale vitamin," B1 strengthens the nervous system and can improve mental attitude. It helps all kinds of stress, so the need for this vitamin increases during illness, trauma, anxiety, and postsurgical periods.

Women who are pregnant, nursing, or taking birth control pills have increased needs for vitamin B1, as do smokers, drinkers, and those who consume a great deal of sugar or caffeine.

Vitamin B1 is water soluble and must be replaced daily.

Benefits

- necessary in treatment of *beriberi, neuritis,* and *alcoholism*

- *aids digestion,* particularly of carbohydrates

- helps fight *air- or seasickness*

- *maintains* normal functioning of the nervous system, *muscles, heart*

- aids in *treatment* of herpes zoster (shingles)

- helps relieve *dental postoperative pain*

- promotes *growth*

- improves *mental attitude*

- repels *biting insects*

Natural sources:

Whole wheat, oatmeal, peanuts, bran, most vegetables, milk, rice husks, dried yeast, brewer's yeast, and blackstrap molasses.

VITAMIN B2 (RIBOFLAVIN)

Vitamin B2 helps the body digest fats, proteins, and carbohydrates and convert them into energy it can use.

Those who may be deficient in this vitamin include people who habitually skip meals, refuse to eat liver or green vegetables, or follow a restrictive diet (as for ulcers, colitis, or diabletes) over a long period of time. Alcoholism may also lead to B2 deficiency.

Vitamin B2 must be replaced daily.

Benefits

- helps clear up *lesions* of the *mouth, lips, skin, genitalia* benefits *vision,* alleviates *eye fatigue,* prevents *twilight blindness*

- helps eliminate *sore mouth, lips, tongue*

- promotes healthy *skin, nails, hair*

- aids in *growth and reproduction*

- functions with other substances to *metabolize* carbohydrates, fats, proteins

- aids in *stress situations*

Natural Sources

Liver, kidney, fish, eggs, cheese, milk, yeast, leafy green vegetables, brewer's yeast, blackstrap molasses.

VITAMIN B3 (NIACIN)

Vitamin B3 is necessary for a healthy nervous system and proper brain function. A lack of this vitamin can cause negative personality changes.

Vitamin B3 is also essential for the body to produce cortisone, thyroxine, insulin, and male and female sex hormones.

The body can usually produce its own vitamin B3, but only if it is receiving enough vitamins B1, B2, and B6.

If you are taking extra vitamin B3, you may notice a flushing and itching of the skin - this is normal and should not last long

Vitamin B3 must be replaced daily.

Benefits

- combats *pellagra, confusion, digestive difficulties,* and *blotched skin;* relieves such symptoms as *perceptual changes* ("hearing things" or "seeing things" that aren't there).

- counteracts *arteriosclerosis* (hardening of the arteries)

- *reduces cholesterol*

- increases circulation and *reduces high blood pressure*

- helps prevent or make less severe *migraine headaches*

- promotes a *healthy digestive system* and *alleviates digestive problems*

- eliminates *canker sores* and improves *skin's* general *appearance*

- *eases* some attacks of *diarrhea*

- sometimes *helps eliminate bad breath*

Natural sources

Liver, lean meat, kidney, fish, eggs, the white meat of poultry, whole wheat, yeast, wheat germ, roasted peanuts, avocados, dates, figs, prunes.

VITAMIN B5 (PANTOTHENIC ACID)

Vitamin B5 is necessary in the production of various hormones.

It is also used to build antibodies and to convert foods into useable energy.

It helps in the production of new cells and the maintenance of normal growth and resistance to stress.

Benefits

- strengthens *adrenals*
- helps control *hypoglycemia*
- aids in preventing *duodenal ulcers*
- fights *infections* and *disease*
- prevents *fatigue*
- aids in healing *wounds*
- speeds recovery after *surgery*
- reduces *negative effects of antibiotics*
- helps prevent *blood and skin disorders*
- eases pain of *arthritis*

Natural sources

Meats, kidney, heart, liver, chicken, nuts, whole grains, wheat germ, bran, yeast, molasses, green vegetables, tomatoes, potatoes.

VITAMIN B6 (PYRIDOXINE)

Vitamin B6 is primarily useful in assuring proper chemical balance in the blood and body tissues. It is essential in helping the body produce niacin (vitamin B3), so a shortage of B6 may be indicated by the symptoms of B3 deficiency.

It also helps the body convert fats and proteins into useful energy, and it helps maintain salt and water balances.

Vitamin B6 is necessary for the production of antibodies and red blood cells.

Those whose diets are high in protein and women who take birth control pills are likely to need extra vitamin B6.

Vitamin B6 must be replaced daily.

Necessary for production of HCL.

Benefits

- Helps treat *anemia*

- alleviates *nausea,* specifically *morning sickness*

- controls *cholesterol* level in blood

- reduces *muscle spasms,* particularly cramps and numbness which occur at night

- promotes healthy *skin, teeth, muscles,* and *nerves*

- helps prevent *kidney and gallstones*

- builds resistance to *ear infections*

- eases *air- and seasickness*

- aid *digestion*

Natural sources

Lean meats, liver, kidney, heart, milk, eggs, soybeans, nuts, yeast, wheat bran, wheat germ, cantaloupe, bananas, molasses, and leafy green vegetables.

VITAMIN B12
(CYANOCOBALAMIN)

Vegetarians risk deficiency in vitamin B12 and so should supplement their diets with this vitamin. Women who are pregnant or nursing also benefit from additional B12.

Because it is sometimes difficult for the body to absorb B12, it should be combined with calcium.

Vitamin B12 is effective in very small doses.

Benefits

- prevents *anemia*
- helps ease *asthma*
- promotes *growth* and increases *appetite* in children
- prevents *eye damage,* particularly from smoke or pollution
- increases *energy*
- relieves *irritability*
- maintains *nervous system*
- aids *digestion*
- helps improve *concentration, memory,* and *balance*

Natural sources

Liver, kidney, beef, saltwater fish, oysters, eggs, milk, cheese.

VITAMIN B13 (OROTIC ACID)

Very little research has yet been done on vitamin B13.

It is not currently available in the United States, but it can be obtained in Europe.

Benefits

- possibly prevents some *liver problems*
- aids in treatment of *multiple sclerosis*
- helps prevent *premature aging*

Natural sources

Root vegetables (carrots, potatoes, turnips, etc.), whey, liquid from curdled milk.

VITAMIN B15 (PANGAMIC ACID)

The essential requirement for vitamin B15 has not been proved. It is enthusiastically used in Russia, but the U.S. Food and Drug Administration has given some resistance to its sale in the United States.

Some people become slightly nauseated for a little while after starting to take B15, but this usually lasts only a few days. Taking the vitamin after the day's largest meal helps ease this nausea.

B15 acts more effectively if taken together with vitamins A and E.

Russians recommend taking 50 mg three times a day for 90 days, cutting back then to one a day.

Benefits

- stops the *craving for liquor*
- speeds recovery from *fatigue*
- protects against *pollutants*
- helps lower *cholesterol* level
- increases *immunity* to infections
- relieves symptoms of *angina* and *asthma*
- helps prevent *cirrhosis*
- aids in easing *hangovers*
- *mental disorders*

Natural sources

Whole grains, whole brown rice, pumpkin seeds, sesame seeds, yeast.

VITAMIN B17 (LAETRILE)

Vitamin B17 is very controversial. It has been rejected by the U.S. Food and Drug Administration, and its use in cancer treatment is legal only in parts of the United States.

Massive doses of B17 should never be taken all at once. It is better to take small doses at different times during the day. It is recommended to take in addition to B17 large doses of vitamin A (in emulsion form) and large doses of enzymes.

Benefits

- may aid in preventing or controlling some *cancers*

Natural sources

The pits of apricots, cherries, peaches, plums, nectarines, apples, and various types of seeds.

VITAMIN B FACTORS (INOSITOL)

Inositol seems to be most effective when taken together with other vitamins, particularly vitamin E, choline, and biotin.

Inositol appears to be important in the proper function of the heart, eyes, and brain.

Benefits

- prevents *eczema*

- promotes healthy *hair* and helps prevent *hair loss*

- regulates *cholesterol levels* and aids in treatment of *atherosclerosis*

- aids in redistribution of *body fat*

- builds resistance to *cirrhosis of the liver*

- helps in treatment of *nerve damage* from some types of *muscular dystrophy*

- counteracts *negative effects of caffeine*

- *constipation*

Natural sources

Organ meats (liver, heart, brains), peanuts, dried lima beans, yeast, molasses, wheat germ, raisins, cantaloupe, grapefruit, cabbage.

VITAMIN B FACTORS (CHOLINE)

Choline is necessary in liver development and in maintaining the functions of both liver and kidney.

It is also required in the thin covering of nerve fibers - a deficiency of choline can damage the nerves and so impair body functions.

Benefits

- helps control *cholesterol*
- sustains healthy *nerves, kidneys, liver*
- maintains *muscles*
- helps control *blood pressure*
- aids those nerve impulses that effect *memory*
- assists liver in *eliminating poisons* from the blood

Natural sources

Organ meats, egg yolks, yeast, wheat germ, peanuts or peanut butter, green leafy vegetables, various seeds, soybeans, and fish.

VITAMIN B FACTORS
(FOLIC ACID)

Folic acid is most effective when taken together with vitamin B12. In turn, it is necessary for the full effectiveness of vitamins A, D, E, and K.

Those who should increase their folic acid intake include people who take large doses of vitamin C, women who are pregnant (particularly just before delivery) or nursing, women who take birth control pills, and persons who drink alcoholic beverages.

Benefits

- helps prevent *anemia*
- improves *lactation*
- aids in reducing *pain*
- protects against *intestinal parasites and food poisoning*
- sometimes helps delay the *graying of hair* (when used with pantothenic acid and PABA)
- increases *appetite* in those who are run down
- promotes healthy-looking *skin*
- helps prevent *canker sores*
- aids in *atherosclerosis*

Natural sources

Liver, egg yolks, yeast, bran, avocados, pumpkins, cantaloupe, apricots, whole wheat, dark rye flour, deepgreen leafy vegetables, carrots.

VITAMIN C (ASCORBIC ACID)

Vitamin C is essential for the body to produce collagen, which is the substance that bonds cells together. Maintaining vitamin C in your body therefore helps preserve and mend the connective tissues (tendons and cartilage - including the cartilage between spinal discs), bones, muscles, and blood vessels.

Vitamin C also helps the body use iron.

You need extra vitamin C if you:
—smoke
—take aspirin often
—live or work in a city or other environment with carbon monoxide in the air
—take birth control pills.

Vitamin C must be replaced daily.

Benefits

- prevents *scurvy*

- helps prevent or make less severe the *common cold*

- promotes healing of *wounds, burns, and bone fractures*

- increases resistance to *infections, fatigue,* and *low temperatures*

- aids in prevention of *internal bleeding,* from *ulcers* to simple *bruises*

- helps guard against *anemia*

- maintains solid *bones* and *teeth*
- promotes healthy *gums*
- helps relieve *back problems and related discomforts*

- acts as a mild *diuretic*

- helps body meet various *stresses*

- encourages healing after *surgery*

- aids in decreasing *cholesterol* level in the blood

- reduces discomforts of *allergies*

- gives a high resistance to *cancer*

- fights also against *cataracts, cystitis, pyorrhea, aging, diabetes, and gallstones*

Natural sources

Citrus fruits (oranges, grapefruit, lemons, limes, tomatoes), green leafy vegetables, broccoli, cauliflower, berries, cantaloupe, potatoes.

VITAMIN D

Vitamin D is necessary for the body to build calcium in the bones. It is also required to release the calcium for the body's use. Because of this, vitamin D deficiency is usually related to calcium deficiency conditions.

We can receive vitamin D directly from the sunshine as well as through diet. Those whose clothing, environment, or work schedules limit their exposure to the sum should probably increase the vitamin D in their diets. It should be noted that once a suntan is established, the skin no longer absorbs vitamin D from the sun.

Women who are pregnant or nursing need extra vitamin D, as do children who are still growing.

Benefits

- prevents *rickets*

- helps prevent *osteomalacia* and some *irregularities in heartbeat*

- builds strong *bones* and *teeth*

- aids in producing *blood plasma*

- is effective in treatment of *keratoconus (distention of the cornea)*

- relieves *chronic conjunctivitis*

- prevents *colds* when taken with vitamins A and C

- helps body use *calcium, phosphorus and vitamin A*

Natural sources

Milk, dairy products, ultraviolet sun rays, egg yolk, fish liver oils, sardines, herring, salmon, tuna.

VITAMIN E

Vitamin E acts to control the unsaturated fatty acids in the body; it affects virtually all body tissues.

Vitamin E is more potent when taken together with selenium.

Vitamin E boosts the action of vitamin A.

Those who drink chlorinated water and women who are pregnant, nursing, taking birth control pills, or going through the menopause need extra vitamin E.

Vitamin E may be applied directly in treatment of wounds or other skin disorders.

Vitamin E should be replaced regularly.

Benefits

- strengthens and protects *reproductive, muscular, circulatory, skeletal,* and *nervous systems*

- improves *circulation*

- helps prevent *arteriosclerosis* and *blood clots*

- useful in treating *gangrene, nephritis, rheumatic fever, purpura, retinitis, diabetes mellitus, congenital heart disease, phlebitis*

- prevents or lessens *scar tissue,* both internal and external, and so is helpful after surgery or *heart attack*

- aids healing of *wounds, burns, chronic ulcers,* and *some skin diseases*

- protects *respiratory system* from *pollution*

- increases *fertility*

- prevents *premature aging*

- improves *endurance*

- acts as mild *diuretic* (and may therefore lower *blood pressure*)

- helps prevent *miscarriage*

- counteracts *fatigue*

- strengthens *heart*
- carries *oxygen*
- goes straight to *placenta*

Natural sources

Wheat germ, vegetable oils, peanuts, whole-grain cereals, green leafy vegetables, broccoli, spinach, eggs.

VITAMIN F (UNSATURATED FATTY ACIDS)

The unsaturated fatty acids provide the body with fats in a form which can be used. They also aid in burning up the saturated fats already in the system.

Vitamin F is best absorbed if taken with vitamin E.

Those whose diets include a great deal of carbohydrates need additional vitamin F.

Benefits

- prevents *eczema* and *acne*

- aids in *weight reduction*

- helps control *cholesterol* levels

- encourages healthy *hair* and *skin*

- provides some protection against *negative effects of x-rays*

Natural sources

Oils of wheat germ, linseed, corn, cottonseed, sunflower, safflower, soybean, and peanut; walnuts, almonds, pecans, peanuts, avocados.

LECITHIN

Major sources of Lecithin are soybeans, though traces are also found in all vegetable oils, such as corn and wheat germ oil. Soybean is most desirable because of its high protein content and availability.

Benefits

- Breaks down *fat and cholesterol*
- *Brain food*
- Lowers *blood pressure*
- Increases *gamma globulin* in the blood
- Helps *fight infection*
- Skin disturbances such as *eczema, acne and psoriasis*
- Softens *aging skin*
- Natural *tranquilizer*
- *Sexual aid*
- Helpful in *weight loss*
- Helpful in *assimilation of vitamins A and E*
- Combination of vitamin E and Lecithin found useful in *lowering the requirements of insulin in diabetics*

Lecithin becomes rancid very easily and should be kept refrigerated at all times. If it becomes rancid, it can do more harm than good. One of the safest ways of taking Lecithin is in the form of gelatin capsules as they have been hermetically sealed, giving extra protection against the problem of rancidity.

VITAMIN H (BIOTIN)

Vitamin H helps the liver produce lipids (fats) and promotes the conversion of food into energy.   Vitamin H is necessary to utilize vitamin C.   Raw egg whites counteract vitamin H, so those who eat or drink mixtures containing raw egg should increase their vitamin H.

Benefits

- helps prevent *eczema*
- eases *muscle pain*
- aids *metabolism*
- helps prevent *baldness* and *graying of hair*
- builds resistance to some *allergies*
- alleviates or prevents *exhaustion*

Natural sources

Green leafy vegetables, nuts, fruits, unrefined rice, egg yolks, liver, kidney, milk.

VITAMIN K

Besides its uses in the human body, vitamin K works as an excellent preservative for food. It does not alter the taste or appearance of the food it preserves.

Benefits

- helps prevent *colitis*
- promotes adequate *blood clotting*
- reduces susceptibility to *nose bleeds*
- works to counteract *nausea* in pregnant women
- reduces excessive *menstrual flow*
- prevents *internal hemorrhaging*
- aids in treating *snakebite*
- helps relieve *pain*

Natural sources

Yogurt, green leafy vegetables, root vegetables (carrots, potatoes, turnips), alfalfa, safflower oil, soybean oil, kelp.

VITAMIN P (BIOFLAVONOIDS)

Vitamin P is essential for the proper absorption and use of vitamin C. These two vitamins work together to strengthen capillaries and connective tissues.

When you buy *natural* vitamin C, you usually get vitamin P as well.

Two well-known members of this Bioflavonoid complex are Rutin and Hesperidin.

Benefits

- prevents *bruising*
- helps treat *edema* and *dizziness* which result from *inner ear infections*
- builds resistance to *infections*
- prevents *bleeding gums*
- helps prevent *miscarriage*
- helps to *build immunity to cancer*
- eases and speeds recovery from *influenza* and the *common cold*
- helps counteract *hemorrhages* caused by *anticoagulant drugs*
- *boost action of vitamin C*

Natural sources

Citrus fruits (primarily the white skin and the segment membranes), apricots, blackberries, cherries, grapes, plums, rose hips.

PABA

PABA helps the body make folic acid and use pantothenic acid (vitamin B5).

It is destroyed by some antibiotics and sulfa drugs, so PABA intake should be increased while taking those medications.

Benefits

- helps prevent *eczema*

- aids in healing and relieving pain of *burns*

- keeps *skin* healthy and helps prevent *wrinkles*

- screens the sun and prevents *sunburn* when applied directly to the skin

- helps restore *natural hair color*

Natural sources

Organ meats (liver, kidney), yeast, whole grains, wheat germ, bran.

VITAMIN T

Very little research has been done for this vitamin.

Benefits

- helps *blood coagulation*
- prevents some kinds of *anemia* and *hemophilia*

Natural sources

Egg yolks, sesame seeds.

VITAMIN U

Little is known about this vitamin.

Benefits

- helps heal *ulcers* (peptic and duodenal ulcers)

Natural sources

Raw cabbage

Minerals

Minerals are necessary to regulate body functions and to maintain tissues. Minerals, as well as vitamins, must be supplied daily either in the diet or through supplements.

Minerals are necessary for the body to be able to use vitamins. Minerals are the spark plugs of vitamin use. You can see that this chain of digestive chemical reactions is complicated and interrelated. Without vitamins and minerals you could eat everything in sight and still be malnourished.

To complicate things further, minerals cannot be used by the body unless they have been broken down into a digestible form. This process is called chelation (pronounced *key'lation*), and it frequently costs you up to half the amount of minerals you take. Because of this, it is both cheaper and wiser to purchase mineral supplements in chelated form. Cutting this one step out of the work your body has to do to use the fuel you feed it makes a big difference in the effectiveness of the nutritional process.

Research done in Poland has shown that vitamins and minerals put in a base of herbs will raise the body's ability to use those vitamins and minerals four-to-five times better than it would be able to without the herbs. This is a form of natural chelation; any vitamin and mineral product assembled this way is naturally chelated.

Vitamins are organic. That is, they are built of chemical structures based on carbon. But minerals are not basically carbons (with the exception of a few organic irons). Just the right combinations of vitamins and minerals are very important. Keep the following guidelines in mind as you plan your balanced diet.

CALCIUM

Calcium and phosphorus should be balanced two-to-one in the human body.

Vitamin D is necessary for proper use of calcium.

Growing children and hypoglycemics benefit from increased calcium intake.

Calcium helps the body use iron.

Benefits

- prevents *rickets*

- promotes growth and maintenance of healthy *teeth and bones*

- maintains *cardiovascular system,* including regulating *heart beat*

- supports *nervous system,* particularly transmission of *nerve impulses;* calms nerves

- increases a person's *ability to withstand pain*

- relieves *muscle spasms*

- relieves *menstrual cramps*

- helps treat *insomnia*

- eases *"growing pains"*

- nothing *heals* without enough *calcium*

Natural sources

Milk and dairy products, cheese, peanuts, sunflower seeds, walnuts, soybeans, dried beans, green vegetables, salmon, sardines.

CHROMIUM

Benefits

- helps prevent *diabetes*
- deters *arteriosclerosis*
- aids *growth*
- helps prevent and correct *high blood pressure*

Natural sources

Meat, shellfish, clams, chicken, corn oil, yeast.

CHLORINE

Most people who eat an average amount of sea salt each day get adequate chlorine.

Those whose water is chlorinated should eat yogurt to restore intestinal bacteria. They should also increase their intake of vitamin C and vitamin E.

Benefits

- promotes healthy *teeth* and *hair*
- aids *digestion*

Natural sources

Sea salt, olives, kelp.

COBALT

Very strict vegetarians are likely to need supplementary cobalt.

Benefits

- helps prevent *anemia*
- builds *red blood cells*

Natural sources

Meat, kidney, liver, clams, oysters, milk.

COPPER

Most people who eat balanced diets get adequate copper. Supplementary copper is rarely prescribed and care should be taken not to over-treat oneself with it. Excessive amounts of copper can keep you awake at night, cause irregular menstrual periods, bring on depression, or increase hair loss.

Copper is required for the body to make proper use of iron and vitamin C.

Benefits

- maintain *high enerey level*
- helps prevent *anemia* and *edema*

Natural sources

Whole wheat, dried beans, peas, liver, shrimp, most seafood, prunes.

FLUORINE

Synthetic fluorine is a toxic poison in water, vitamins, and toothpaste. Natural fluorine is beneficial to the body. An excess of either natural or synthetic fluorine can cause mottling or discoloration to the teeth. Fluorine is an essential trace mineral concentrated in the teeth and bones. It helps the body in the use of calcium.

Benefits

- strengthens *bones*
- builds resistance to *tooth decay*

Natural sources

Seafoods, gelatin, whole wheat, garlic, beets, lettuce, cabbage, radishes, egg whites.

IODINE

Sufficient iodine for most people is supplied in regular multivitamin and mineral tablets. Those who live in regions where the soil is iodine-poor (the Midwest, for example) and women who are pregnant or nursing might need more.

Benefits

- helps prevent *goiter* and *hypothyroidism*
- encourages *growth*
- boosts *energy level*
- helps system *burn excess fat*
- aids in maintaining *mental alertness* and the ability to *think quickly*
- promotes healthy *hair, skin, teeth,* and *nails*
- promotes *healthy tonsils,* which are part of the lymphatic and immune system.

Natural sources

Seafood, kelp, vegetables grown in rich soil.

IRON

Iron is necessary for the body to absorb and use B vitamins.

In turn, vitamin C and copper, cobalt, and manganese must be present for the body to use iron.

Those who should take extra iron include menstruating women and those who drink large amounts of coffee or tea.

Benefits

- prevents and helps treat *anemia*
- promotes *growth*
- builds *resistance to disease*
- restores healthy *skin tone*
- guards against *fatigue*

Natural sources

Red meat, organ meats (liver, kidney, heart), egg yolks, clams, oysters, dried peaches, nuts, beans, asparagus, oatmeal.

MAGNESIUM

Magnesium is essential for the body to be able to use calcium and vitamin C.

It helps convert blood sugar into usable energy.

Women who take birth control pills and anyone who drinks alcohol should increase their magnesium.

Since magnesium neutralizes stomach acids, it should not be taken directly after a meal.

Benefits

- helps prevent *heart attack* and keeps the *cardiovascular system* healthy

- relieves *indigestion*

- aids in resisting *depression*

- helps prevent *calcium deposits* and *kidney stones and gallstones*

- improves *dental health*

- *relaxes muscle*

Natural sources

Yellow corn, dark green vegetables, lemons, grapefruit, figs, nuts, seeds, apples.

MANGANESE

Those who drink a great deal of milk or eat a large amount of meat may need additional manganese.

Benefits

- promotes proper *development and function of central nervous system, thyroid hormones,* and *skeletal and reproductive systems*
- required in *digestion* and *metabolism* of food
- Improves *reflexes*
- reduces *irritability*
- eliminates *fatigue*
- improves *memory*

Natural sources

Whole-grain cerials, nuts, peas, green leafy vegetables, beets, egg yolks.

MOLYBDENUM

Molybdenum helps the body convert food into usable energy. It also contributes to the utilization of iron.

Most people get adequate molybdenum in their diets.

Benefits

- helps prevent *anemia*

Natural sources

Dark green leafy vegetables, peas, beans, nuts, whole grains.

PHOSPHORUS

Phosphorus requires calcium (ratio 1-to-2) in order to work.
Vitamin D is also necessary for phosphorus to be effective.

Benefits

- prevents *rickets* and *pyorrhea*
- builds healthy *bones and teeth*
- aids regular *heartbeat* and normal *kidney function*
- decreases *arthritis* pain
- promotes general *growth* and *healing* of tissues

Natural sources

Fish, poultry, meat, eggs, seeds, nuts, whole grains.

POTASSIUM

Conditions which may indicate need for additional potassium include hypoglycemia, severe diarrhea, mental or physical stress, long periods of fasting or dieting. The increase of the use of salt as a preservative has increased the need for potassium.

Benefits

- aids in skin's *elasticity*
- helps keep *heart rhythms* normal
- aids in regulating body's *water balance*
- encourages *clear thinking*
- helps control *allergies*
- aids in disposal of *body wastes*
- helps reduce *blood pressure*
- aids in *slowing aging*

Natural sources

Citrus fruits, green leafy vegetables, watercress, mint leaves, sunflower seeds, bananas, potatoes.

SELENIUM

Selenium works best in combination with vitamin E.
    In general, men need a little more selenium than women do.

Benefits

- slows down *aging* process
- prevents *heart* disease
- maintains *elasticity* in tissues
- helps treat and prevent *dandruff*
- provides protection from certain *cancer*
- combats *harmful metals* in our environment

Natural sources

Bran, wheat germ, tuna, tomatoes, onions, broccoli.

SILICON

Found in high concentrations in the hair, skin and nails.

Benefits

- promotes *healing*
- promotes *growth of nails* and *hair*
- stops *splitting* of nails and hair
- aids in the *retention* and *utilization* of calcium
- aids in the *retention* of B vitamins
- aids in *sweating*

Natural sources

Skins of fruits and vegetables, horsetail, gelatin.

SODIUM

Most people eat much more salt than they realize or than they need to eat. It is easier to add sodium to your diet than to eliminate or cut down on it.

An excess of sodium may contribute to high blood pressure.

It is recommended that most people cut their salt intake. However, for those *few* who need extra salt, kelp is an ideal supplement.

Benefits

- prevents *sunstroke* and *heat prostration*
- aids in proper function of *muscles and nerves*
- promotes *digestion of carbohydrates*
- in some cases helps prevent *neuralgia*

Natural sources Natural sources

Sea salt, shellfish, carrots, beets, artichokes, dried beef.

SULFUR

Most people whose diet includes adequate protein are also getting enough sulfur.

Benefits

- promotes healthy *hair, skin, nails*
- applied creams, helps treat various *skin problems*
- maintains oxygen balance for proper *brain function*
- supports the *liver* in bile secretion
- helps combat *bacterial infections*

Natural sources

Beef, fish, eggs, dried beans, cabbage.

VANADIUM

Vanadium taken in synthetic form can easily be toxic. However, it is rarely needed as a supplement.

Benefits

- cuts down formation of *cholesterol* in blood vessels
- helps prevent *heart attack*

Natural sources

Fish.

ZINC

Alcoholics, diabetics, and those who take large doses of vitamin B6 need to increase their zinc intake.

Those who take extra zinc should also take extra vitamin A.

Benefits

- prevents *prostate* problems
- helps control *cholesterol* deposits and so prevents *arteriosclerosis*
- contributes to the formation of *insulin*
- aids in *healing of wounds,* both internal and external
- promotes *growth* and *mental alertness*
- restores *sense of taste and smell*
- helps treat *infertility*
- eliminates *white spots on fingernails*
- may help regulate *menstrual periods*
- combats against *impotency*
- fights against *tinnitus*
- helps prevent *hearing loss*
- helps prevent *hair loss*
- helps to make *fragile nails* stronger
- fights against *adult acne*
- helps to make *rough skin* smoother

Natural sources

Eggs, yeast, wheat germ, nonfat dry milk, ground mustard, pumpkin seeds, fish.

WATER

Water is often a forgotten element essential to proper health. Most people would benefit by increasing their daily water intake.

Thirst is the body's way of telling us that more water is needed. Extra glasses of water taken regularly throughout the day (and not just when one feels thirsty) would help people.

Drink plenty of water! An ideal amount would be to drink about one glass of liquid (water) every two hours. For dieters, drink a full glass before each meal.

Benefits

- helps *keep all systems functioning*

- regulates body *temperature*

- prevents *constipation*

- aids in *dieting* by depressing appetite before meals

- prevents *dehydration*

- helps the body combat *fever, disease,* and *infection* by ridding it of impurities

- prevents the formation of *kidney stones*

- keeps the *digestive tract functioning* properly

Natural sources

Drinking water, juices, fruits, vegetables, reverse osmosis water. Fruits are 90 percent distilled water. Bottled water and filtered water are sometimes questionable as to their source and the effectiveness of longivity of the filter.

One of the best ways to get purified water is through the use of Reverse Osmosis units that can be utilized in the home. Even the pharaceutical people use Reverse Osmosis (R. O.) units in the making of drugs and baby formulas. Our astronauts have to reuse all water when in space so all their water is purified

Vitamins & Minerals from Herbal Sources

Many of the vitamins and minerals our bodies need can be obtained in natural forms - through herbs. Herbs are highly respected for their healing qualities. When a person takes them for vitamin and mineral content as well, he's getting double benefit.

It may be that a major reason why herbs are so effective in body healing is that they *are* high in vitamins and minerals. We've included this section of the book for those who are concerned with natural health and who would like to obtain their vitamins and minerals from the most natural source there is, the herbs that Mother Earth freely gives to us.

In this section we've listed some of the most popular herbs and their reported vitamin and mineral content. You can determine elsewhere in the book which vitamins and minerals your body needs. Then, if desired, you can get what you need from the herbs we've listed.

While you're at it, you may want to see how herbs use vitamins and minerals to do their work. Using this section, look up the herb you're interested in. See what vitamins and minerals it contains. Then move to the other sections of the book to see how those vitamins and minerals benefit the body. In that way you'll be able to better see how they assist the herb in its work as a healing agent, (Should you desire more information on herbs, we refer you to the companion volume of this book, *The Little Herb Encyclopedia, Revised,* published by Woodland Books.)

No one really knows *how* the body uses vitamins and minerals in its effort to keep healthy. We do know that they are essential for healthy living. We know that the body deteriorates and becomes sick if it doesn't have them - and can even die. And we know that they have certain medicinal properties that the body is able to utilize.

Herbs are much the same way. They have the ability to keep us healthy, even though often times we don't know precisely how they work. But we do know they *do* work - and thousands of years of use has demonstrated that over and over again.

By combining our knowledge of the vitamin and mineral content of herbs with our understanding of many of the health benefits of those vitamins and minerals, we're able to come much closer to our goal of using the right things for the right reasons. As you use this section about the earth's natural healers you'll be able to approach that goal for yourself.

VITAMIN A

alfalfa, burdock, capsicum, dandelion, garlic, kelp, marshmallow, papaya, parsley, pokeweed, raspberry, red clover, safflower, watercress, and yellow dock.

VITAMIN B1 (Thiamine)

capsicum, dandelion, fenugreek, kelp, parsley, safflower, raspberry.

VITAMIN B2 (Riboflavin)

alfalfa, burdock, dandelion, fenugreek, kelp, safflower, watercress.

VITAMIN B3 (Niacin)

alfalfa, burdock, dandelion, fenugreek, kelp, parsley, sage.

VITAMIN B6 (Pyridoxine)

alfalfa.

VITAMIN B12 (Cyanocobalamin)

alfalfa, kelp.

VITAMIN C

alfalfa, burdock, boneset, catnip, capsicum, chickweed, dandelion, garlic, hawthorne, horseradish, kelp, lobelia, parsley, plantain, pokeweed, papaya, rose hips, shepherd's purse, strawberry, watercress, yellow dock.

VITAMIN D

alfalfa, watercress.

VITAMIN E

alfalfa, dandelion, kelp, raspberry, rose hips, watercress.

VITAMIN G

alfalfa, capsicum, dandelion, gotu kola, kelp.

VITAMIN K

alfalfa.

VITAMIN P (Rutin)

dandelion, rose hips.

VITAMIN T

plantain, alfalfa.

VITAMIN U

alfalfa.

ALUMINUM

alfalfa.

CALCIUM

alfalfa, blue cohosh, chamomile, capsicum, dandelion, horsetail, Irish moss, kelp, mistletoe, nettle, parsley, plantain, pokeweed, pumpkin seeds, raspberry, rose hips, shepherd's purse, yellow dock, watercress.

CHLOROPHYLL

alfalfa.

CHLORINE

alfalfa, dandelion, kelp, parsley, raspberry.

COPPER

kelp, parsley, watercress.

FLUORINE

garlic, alfalfa.

IODINE

dulse, garlic, Irish moss, kelp, sarsaparilla, black walnut, dandelion.

IRON

alfalfa, burdock, blue cohosh, capsicum, dandelion, dulse, kelp, mullein, nettle, parsley, pokeweed, red beet, rhubarb, rose hips, strawberry leaves, yellow dock.

LITHIUM

kelp.

MAGNESIUM

alfalfa, blue cohosh, capsicum, dandelion, kelp, mistletoe, mullein, peppermint, primrose, raspberry, watercress, willow, wintergreen.

MANGANESE

kelp.

PHOSPHORUS

alfalfa, blue cohosh, caraway, capsicum, chickweed, dandelion, garlic, Irish moss, kelp, licorice, parsley, pokeweed, raspberry, rose hips, watercress, yellow dock.

POTASSIUM

alfalfa, blue cohosh, chamomile, comfrey, dulse, dandelion, eyebright, fennel, Irish moss, kelp, mistletoe, nettle, papaya, parsley, peppermint, plantain, raspberry, shepherd's purse, white oak bark, yarrow, wintergreen.

SELENIUM

alfalfa, kelp.

SILICON

alfalfa, blue cohosh, burdock, horsetail, kelp, nettle.

SODIUM

alfalfa, dandelion, dulse, fennel, Irish moss, kelp, mistletoe, parsley, shepherd's purse.

SULFUR

alfalfa, burdock, capsicum, eyebright, fennel, garlic, Irish moss, kelp, mullein, nettle, parsley, plantain, raspberry, sage, shepherd's purse, thyme.

ZINC

kelp, marshmallow, licorice, ginseng, ho shou wu, damiana.

TRACE MINERALS

alfalfa, kelp. (boron, brominem nickel, strontium, vanadium)

Bach Flower Remedies

About 1976 we were introduced to Bach Flower Remedies. We wondered about them and, like all facets of health that we have been introduced to, began to check it out and use them ourselves. Well, over the years we have used them to help many people as well as our family!

Dr. Edward Bach

Dr. Bach was a highly respected physician in England in the early 1930's and he became convinced, after many years of research and practice, that many of his patients' illnesses were the direct manifestation of mental and emotional stress. He excelled in many areas of medicine in his 20 years of practice. He was a pathologist, bacteriologist and immunologist.

In 1920, through his research in bacteriology, he concluded that certain strains of bacteria found in the intestinal tract were the primary cause of most chronic illnesses. He then developed a series of vaccines which were highly successful in alleviating a wide variety of chronic disorders. Although many orthodox medical doctors hailed his vaccines as a major medical breakthrough, Dr. Bach was not happy with many of the side effects. Shortly, therefore, he was introduced to the field of homeopathy and found that by preparing the vaccines as homeopathic remedies, the side effects were substantially reduced. They were called the Bach nosodes and proved to be a major step forward and many homeopathic physicians came to regard Dr. Bach as one of the foremost contributors to the field of homeopathy since Samual Hahnemann, its founder.

Dr. Bach found that by treating the personality it was a very important factor in curing of illness. He continued with his research and concluded that disease was the consolidation of mental attitudes, the physical manifestation of various negative states of mind. Dr. Bach rejected all his previous work as not addressing the real issues of health and the cure of disease. He gave up his prosperous Harley Street practice and set out for the Welsh countryside, convinced that the simple plants of the field would provide the essential elements necessary to restore health and vitality.

During the time 1930 to 1936 Dr. Bach discovered 38 flowering trees, plants, and special waters, which were used to treat such negative states of mind as uncertainty, impatience, and fear. One need only to identify the state of mind, mood, or personality type and then pick the appropriate flower remedy to match it. These essences are today known as the **Bach Flower Remedies.**

Dr. Bach used extensive research and found the remedies to be completely safe for use, requiring the smallest dosages to be effective. In addition, it was reported the the Bach Flower Remedies would not interfere with or be affected by any other form of medicine a person might be required to take; if improperly chosen they would, at worst, show a lack of effectiveness; and if taken in overdosage, will do no harm.

There are some modern day practitioners who are experimenting with other flowers as remedies also. They are at this date still trying and proving these new remedies, so Dr. Bach's work goes on in this day and age. One such group is based in California and called the Flower Essence Service. They have come upon many new flowers to be used as an aid to emotional problems.

Be assured that Flower Essences are from a homeopathic origin and are so designed to help the body, not hinder it, following the principle of "like cures like."

The list that follows has been designed to help you understand not only the reason we would use the Flower Essences, but the results you would hope to achieve from the use of them

Flower Essence

Negative Side		Positive Side
Hide problems and worries deep within. Sleeplessness. Sometimes resorts to drugs or alcohol to dull mental torture.	**Agrimony**	Laugh at worries that are unimportant; optimist; peacemaker.
Unknown Fear bringing terror, anxiety and even panic without the least reason.	**Aspen**	Fearless; deep Faith, feel great joy for life.
Lack of humility; critical; not able to put oneself in another person's place. Passing judgment.	**Beech**	Forgiving; deep understanding of people; tolerant.
Quiet; timid; docile; submissive; easily imposed upon by others.	**Centaury**	Serves wisely, quietly, unobtrusively; keeps individuality; follows higher dictate of inner self.
Follows advice of others against his own good judgment. Talkative; saps vitality of others with questions.	**Cerato**	Quiet assurance; very intuitive; can judge between right and wrong; trusts in himself.
Fear of losing control of thought or actions. Thought of suicide.	**Cherry Plum**	Calm, quiet courage under pressure; much endurance.
Make same mistakes over and over again. Does not learn from experience.	**Chestnut Bud**	Good student; learns from own experiences and example of others.
Outward flow of love is blocked and turned inward. Is over possessive of others. Tries to control and direct others.	**Chicory**	Selfless in care and concern for others; gives without thought of return.
Avoids difficulties or unpleasantness by withdrawing into own world. Listless, apathetic and inattentive.	**Clematis**	Lively interest in life; practical idealist. Master of own thoughts.
The mind needs cleansing of that which it takes, and that which fills it with despair and disgust.	**Crab Apple**	Complete control of thoughts; wise, broad-minded; can transmute disharmony into harmony.
Occasionally feels overwhelmed by responsibilities and scope of work. Feels results of efforts are inadequate; this brings on a state of despondency and exhaustion.	**Elm**	Self-assurance; confidence. Good leader. Unshakable inner conviction. helps other people.
Negative outlook. Suffers from deep depression and dark melancholia. Easily discouraged.	**Gentian**	No thought of failure; no obstacle too great; no task too big.
Has lost heart and hope. Feels it is useless to try any more. Has given up.	**Gorse**	Positive faith and hope; certain to overcome all difficulties in the end.
Concerned about self. Filled with problems, difficulties and trivia of the day. Talks rapidly and incessantly.	**Heather**	Selfless; understanding; willing to listen; unsparing in efforts to help others.
Antidote for hatred. Hatred is absence of love. Hatred breeds insecurity, aggressiveness, jealousy, envy and suspicion. Holly protects us from everything that is not Universal love.	**Holly**	Can give without return. Loving; tolerant; happy; rejoice for another's good fortune.

Negative Side		Positive Side
No interest in the present, no effort to confront existing difficulties. Body left to struggle in present while mind re-lives the past.	Honeysuckle	Retains lessons of the past but lets past negative experiences pass out of the mind.
Fatigue in mind. Doubt of strength or ability to face life or work. Monday Morning Blues.	Hornbeam	Certain of own ability and strength. Can take heavy responsibility.
Active nervous person who moves, eats and speaks quickly. Intelligent and intuitive, good and efficient in whatever they undertake. Impatient with slower people.	Impatians	Geat gentleness and sympathy towards others. Capable; decisive; intuitive; clever; abilities far above average. Tolerant of those who are slower.
Not freightened but convinced he cannot do as well as others. Thinks he might fail.	Larch	Willing to plunge into life. Is not discouraged by failure; know he or she did the best. Doesn't know the word "can't".
Full of fears. Fear of the dark, growing old, heights, illness or loss of job, etc. Normally shy and retiring and prone to hide anxieties.	Mimulus	Faces all trials and difficulties with equanimity and humor. Great understanding and courage.
State of mind is a black depression, almost a hopelessness. Despairing melancholia which comes suddenly and without apparent reason.	Mustard	Unshakeable inner serenity; stability; joy and peace.
Strong physically; can stand great strain. When despair becomes too much - may crack and suffer a nervous breakdown.	Oak	Brave, fighting against great difficulties without loss of hope or slackening of effort. Courage; stability under all conditions.
Fatigue is total; mind and body are drained of strength and there is absolute exhaustion.	Olive	Patient and long suffering. Peace of mind; interest in life.
Self-condemnation; never content with achievements; blames self for not doing better and for mistakes of others.	Pine	Will take responsibility and burdens of others if necessary. Will acknowledge mistakes but not dwell on them. Has great perseverence and humility.
Fear for others, especially family and those dear to them. Always fearing the worst and anticipating misfortune for others.	Red Chestnut	Sends out thoughts of safety, health or courage to those who need them. Remains calm, mentally and physically, during emergency.
Feelings of great alarm or terror because of illness or anything else. Spreads these feelings to other people.	Rock Rose	Courageous, forgetful of self. Will risk life to aid others.
Hard masters on themselves; strict in their way of living. Practices self-denial and self-martyrdom.	Rock Water	Will forsake original theories and beliefs for higher and better truth. Can forgive themselves and others. Experiences joy and peace in life.
Suffers from indecision. Swayed between two things or possibilities. Experiences extremes of joy or sadness, energy or apathy, pessimism or optimism, laughing or crying.	Scleranthus	Calmness and determination. Quick to make a decision and prompt in action. Poise and balance at all times.
Always use in case of an accident, sudden sad news, a bad fright or grievous disappointment. These cause shock as well as unhappiness.	Star of Bethlehem	The comforter and soother of pains and sorrows. If the shock is neutralized, recuperation is accelerated.
Mental torture in the extreme. Terrible, appalling mental dispair. The very soul itself seems to be suffering distruction.	Sweet Chestnut	The kind of Faith that can cause miracles. Desire to help others in despair.
Over-enthusiasm, over-effort, stress and tension. Hold strong opinions and ideas which hardly ever change and which they wish to impose on others.	Vervain	Calm; wise; knows own mind. Allows others the right to opinions. Openminded; listens to others. It is by being rather than doing that great things are accomplished.

Negative Side		Positive Side
Think they know better than anyone else; force their will upon one and all. Demand obedience. Crave power.	**Vine**	Wise; loving; does not dominate; unshakeable confidence and certainty. Helps people to know themselves, and find their path in life.
For advancing stages: teething, puberty. Change -of-life. Big decisions made during life, such as change of occupation, stepping forward in life, leaving old limits and restrictions.	**Walnut**	Constancy and determination. Carry out beliefs and life's work unaffected by adverse circumstances or unhindered by either the opinions or the ridicule of others.
Feel superior to others, and sometimes they are disdainful and condescending. Pride and mental rigidity often manifest themselves in the body as physical stiffness and tension.	**Water Violet**	Tranquil; gentle; sympathetic. Have poise, dignity and pass gracefully through life.
Worry or some depressing happening preys upon the mind. Arguments or words we think we should have said go round and round in the mind	**White Chestnut**	Quiet; calm; controls thoughts and imagination; at peace within and with the world.
Undecided what they should do. Delay in finding life's work. So many ideas and ambitions they cannot come to a decision.	**Wild Oat**	Definite ambitions and goals in life. Allows nothing to interfere with purpose. Life filled with usefulness and happiness.
They become resigned. Feel they have to live with it - it is fate. Do not realize that the power to alter or eliminate conditions lies in their hands.	**Wild Rose**	Lively interest in all happenings; enjoys friends, happiness and good health.
Look upon life with bitterness. Blame everyone but themselves for their misfortunes. Believes their treatment is unjust. Jealous of their fellow man.	**Willow**	Great optimism and faith; sense of humor; see things in right proportion. Forgiveness; kindness.
Use in case of sorrow, sudden bad new, after an accident, shock, fear, terror, panic, any stress or strain.	**Rescue**	Cherry Plum, Clematis, Impatiens, Rock Rose and Star of Bethlehem. "ALWAYS HAVE THE RESCUE ESSENCE ON HAND. THE LIFE YOU SAVE MAY BE YOUR OWN."

Amino Acids

There are approximately 22 amino acids and they are the primary components of protein. There are 8 that are called the Essential Amino Acids.

Tryptophan	Phenylalanine
Leucine	Isoleucine
Lysine	Valine
Methionine	Threonine

They are called "essential" because they cannot be manufactured by the body themselves but must be supplied by foods in the diet.

If one essential amino acid is missing, or is present but in a low amount, protein synthesis in the body will fall to a very low level or stop altogether. If eating a protein food and one of the essential amino acids is in a much lower amount than the others, you will have what is called the limiting amino acid, and that is the factor determining the amount of body protein utilized by the body. For example, if a food contains 100% of a person's Valine requirement but only 20% of his Lysine requirement, it will result in only 20% of the protein in that food being used as protein by the body. The rest will be used as fuel rather than for replenishing of building tissue. Foods such as meat, poultry and dairy products are high in protein content and have a good proportion of essential amino acids. Many vegetables and fruits are low or missing some amino acids, thus rendering the amino acids present relatively useless.

This is one of the reasons why we should not try to live on a mono diet as the combining of foods can balance out our amino acid requirements. Eating a diet constantly deficient or lacking in amino acids can invariably cause rapid aging and disease in the body. Most cancer victims could benefit from the addition of amino acid supplements. The body's protein requirements can be easily met if the foods are properly combined in order to provide useable protein.

We need to emphasize the importance of balancing the amino acids to obtain the best possible protein from foods, Whereas the 8 essential amino acids cannot be manufactured, even in part by the combining of all the nonessential amino acids, the 8 amino acids can manufacture the other 14.

As we are learning more and more about amino acids, we are finding some very startling information. Researchers Durk Pearson and Sandy Shaw have found that a combination of amino acids when taken at bedtime, when the stomach is empty, will help you lose weight while you sleep. These amino acids safely stimulate the release of a growth hormone that boosts the rate at which your body burns fat and builds muscle. Because of increasing your rate of metabolism, you create more muscle and less fat. The growth hormone directs the body to burn fat at a rapid rate, and just as efficiently, build firm, taught muscle tissue. This all-natural formation of amino acids is tryptophan, arginine, ornithine and lysine. Pearson and Shaw point out you could wake up pounds thinner and inches firmer without traditional dieting!

Below is a list of some amino acids and their main functions:

Phenylalanine—it has been claimed that learning may be improved with this amino acid and has proven to be an affective appetite depressant and diet aid. When Phenylalanine with the amino acid known as Aspartic Acid combines, it forms a new sweetener, aspartame. There is some questions, at this time, of brain damage in children when it is taken in large amounts. it is called Nutra-sweet. if you have high blood pressure and are trying to lose weight with the aid of phenylalanine, don't forget to monitor your blood pressure during the period.

Phenylalanine comes in two forms called d and l. L-(Laevo, or left-handed) phenylalanine is the form most commonly found in the high protein foods and is the form the body uses to

96

make its own proteins. D-(dexto, or right-handed) phenylalanine is a nearly identical molecule to the L-form and is found in bacteria and plant tissue. The human body converts D-phenylalanine to L-phenylalanine before it is utilized in known bodily functions.

The role of dl-phenylalanine in the nutritional control of chronic pain-health professionals, Pain Treatment Clinics, and Scientific Research Papers have reported dramatic results in patients with severe, acute and chronic pain conditions including:

Migraine	Postoperative Pain
Neuralgia	Longstanding Whiplash
Joint Pain	Severe Premenstrual "Cramps"
Lower Back Pain	Rheumatoid Arthritis
Depression	Osteoarthritis

D- and dl phenylalanine (DLPA) work by intensifying and prolonging the body's own natural pain-killing response. Essentially, DLPA works because it inhibits endorphin-degrading enzymes so that the endorphis produced by the brain last longer.

DLPA (DL-Phenylalanine) has been found to be 89%-100% effective in the treatment of depression. Studies since 1974 show it to be particularly beneficial in cases of endogenous depression. This is the type of depression that is characterized by a decrease in energy and interest, feelings of worthlessness, and a pervasive sense of helplessness to control the course of one's life. Significant improvement has also been achieved with people suffering reactive depression (thought to be caused by environmental influences such as death in the family) and involutional depression (an aging-related depression). DLPA has also been shown effective in manic-depression, schizophrenic depression, and post-amphetamine depression.

See table 3 on page 118.

Tryptophan — as early as 1913 it was noted that a disease pellagra was due to a deficiency of tryptophan. We know niacin to be the anti-pellagra vitamin and the body can manufacture niacin from dietary tryptophan. This amino acid has been used clinically as an anti-depressant and has been used in PMS (Pre Menstrual Syndrome) with good success. Women with PMS who had clinical signs of severe depression were found to have low levels of tryptophan. Artery or heart spasms can occur in a human being and can cause a heart attack. This type of heart attack accounts for more than 15% of all heart deaths. L-Tryptophan supplements can conceivably reduce the risk of this type of heart attack. L-Tryptophan has also been found to benefit those who have trouble sleeping. It has been found that in the research done in 1979 that L-Tryptophan when used as a sleep aid, it significantly decreased the time necessary to fall asleep. Dr. Ernest Hartman of Boston State Hospital and Tufts University School of Medicine has found that 1,000 milligrams (1 gram) of L-Tryptophan taken 20 minutes prior to going to bed reduces the time required to fall asleep by one-half. It also increased the duration of sleep, and improved the quality of sleep. You certainly don't have to take an "upper" the next day because you took a "downer" the night before. L-Tryptophan does not work by drugging or depressing the central nervous system. L-Tryptophan returns normal function by merely making available for the body to use in making Serotonin. It does not seem to induce sleep during the day, but seems to be very effective at night as it must pass the blood-brain barrier. When taken singly at night, it can do so much more readily if there are no other amino acids trying to get through at the same time. L-Tryptophan and B complex are partners in the body. The body will use some of the L-Tryptophan to make some of the B vitamin Niacin (vitamin B-3) if a person is niacin deficient. Therefore, one may not get the full effect of the L-Tryptophan if one is not getting adequate niacin. One should consider taking a B complex with the L-Tryptophan. Dr. Federigo Sicuteri says it also may be effective in treating migraines. His research showed to be effective in about half of the migraine sufferers treated.

Glutamine (Glutamic Acid) — it is considered to be a nonessential amino acid that has shown it can improve intelligence, speed the healing of ulcers, and give a lift from fatigue. It has also been shown to help control alcoholism, certain types of schizophrenia and the craving of sweets.

Methionine — is a member of the lipotropic team which includes choline, inositol and betaine. Its function primarly, as a lipotropic, it is to prevent excessive fat in the liver. It increases the liver's production of lecithin and helps to prevent cholesterol buildup. It helps prevent disorders to the skin and nails. It also plays an important role as an anti-toxicant and free-radical deactivator. All of these activities help to slow down the aging process. It gives the body the ability to chelate heavy metals and helps to eliminate the buildup of toxic minerals such as lead, mercury, and cadium. It is also classified as an anti-fatigue agent.

Cystein and Cystine — works as an anti-toxicant in the body and works closely with Vitamin E and Selenium. Each of these nutrients enhance the anti-toxicant role of the other. It has been used in the treatment of arthritis, both osteoarthritis and rheumatoid. It is necessary for the utilization of vitamin B6. Cystine protects against the damage from radiation by terminating the free radicals produced by radiation. It is also necessary to have adequate amounts to be able to excrete lead from the tissues. Of course, lead is a toxic heavy metal that can cause irreversible brain damage when allowed to accumulate. Durk Pearson and Sandy Shaw say that Cystine can "extend the life span, increase the growth rate of human hair, and significantly decrease the health risk of smoking and drinking, stimulate the body's disease-fighting immune system, and block reactive hypoglycemia." They caution that you should use three times as much Vitamin C as Cystine. For example, if you take 1,000 mg. of Cystine you should take 3,000 mg. of Vitamin C.

Tryosine — has been found to play a role in controlling anxiety and depression. Dr. Alan J. Glenberg of the Department of Psychiatry of Harvard Medical School has found it will help in mental disorders. Dr. Glenberg reported considerable improvement in two patients whose longstanding depressions were not responsive to conventional drug therapy. An additional note on Tryosine, it is suggested that Tryptophan and Tryosine may be a better sleep aid than Tryptophan alone.

Lysine — one very important function of Lysine is to assure adequate absorption of the mineral Calcium. Another function of this amino acid is to form Collagen. Without Vitamin C or adequate protein to supply the amino acid Lysine, our wounds would not heal properly and we would become more susceptible to infections. One of the new discoveries for Lysine is in the treatment of Herpes Simplex. This viral infection is commonly known as cold sores or fever blisters. Herpes has become a major venereal disease in the United States and can cause serious complications in babies who may contact the disease from the mother during birth. Drs. Chris Kagen and R.W. Tankersley, while working in the viral lab at the Cedars of Lebanon Hospital in Los Angeles, found that the amino acid Lysine inhibited it. They found that Lysine suppressed the symptoms of Herpes in 96% of the 45 patients tested. Several patients were studied for as long as 3 years with complete remission of the Herpes and no adverse reactions observed. Their report stated, "The pain disappeared abruptly overnight in virtually every instance, new vesicles (blisters) failed to appear, and resolution in the majority was considered to be more rapid than in their past experience." Inactive Herpes can be controlled in most individuals with just one 500 mg. tablet of L-Lysine daily, but sometimes a larger dose is needed for the first few months, such as a 500 mg. tablet three times daily from 4 to 6 months.

Treonine —has been known to take on the role of a lipotropic to prevent fatty build-up in the liver.

Histidine — it is necessary for the growth in children and is the amino acid from which a biochemical substance Histamine is derived. Both Histamine and Histidine can chelate such trace elements such as copper and zinc. In some forms of arthritis, there is found an excess of copper and other heavy metals, so it is sometimes used for the treatment of arthritis.

Raw Glandular Concentrates
(Protomorphagens)

In large measure, aging is a function of the health of the glands. If the glands are youthful and if old weak cells are replaced by new strong ones, then the body itself is young. You are only as old as your glands!

When we use raw glandulars, we are using the organ tissue to provide the nutrients that our own organs must have in order to replenish themselves. We use specific glandulars for specific parts of the body, such as brain would supply the proteins, enzymes, vitamins, and other nutritional elements needed to replace brain cells. Adrenal helps the adrenal; liver, liver, etc.

When a pack of wolves kills a deer, or a pride of lions pulls down a zebra, the first parts of the prey they eat are the organs, such as kidney, adrenals, pancreas, thymus, heart, liver, etc. Primitive human hunters followed the same pattern. They ate the organs first and would save the meat for later. They were then assured of getting the best and most concentrated nutrition. In prehistoric times when humans were hunters, a diet rich in organ meat guranteed them necessary nutrition. Even when people settled to the cities, organs remained a very important culinary item. This was also true in the United States until the end of the 19th century, when organs began losing ground to red meat.

The major increase of muscle meat in our diets has been one of the major causes of arthritis and other degenerative diseases, because this type of meat is acid producing. Raw glandulars come from livestock. After the animals have been slaughtered, the organs are removed under carefully controlled conditions and made into the final product which is called a glandular concentrate. It is also called "raw" because it contains all the biological material found in the original tissue which could be destroyed through heat. Europeans have pioneered the therapeutical use of glandular materials. Dr. Paul Niehass, the Dean of Europe's glandular therapists, injected finely ground fresh gland tissue into patients suffering from such diseases as diabetes, premature aging and sexual disfunction. In over 12,000 injections he reported one clinical success after another, sometimes even actually restoring function to glands that had practically ceased to work.

Glandular concentrates have been used in successful treatments for such things as hypoglycemia, prostate cancer and kidney stones. You don't have to wait for disease to strike in order to enjoy the advantages of raw glandulars, nor do you have to endure the pain or expense of cell injections. Laboratory studies using radioactive tagging indicate that the vital factors in glandular material leave the intestines intact and travel through the body through the lymph system. This guarantees that the raw glandular concentrates taken by mouth does deliver effective nutrition to the glands.

Phycicians have for years been injecting liver extracts, expecting, and most of the time receiving, admiral results in many disorders. Some would like to attribute these effects from the iron and the B-complex factors inherent in liver, but when the same quantities of these substances are used alone, the results are not the same.

It is believed that glandular tissue concentrates in some way transmit specific DNA stimulants. DNA (Deoxyribonucleic Acid) is the master chemical blueprint for building of new cells, and the RNA (Ribonucleic Acid) is the messenger chemical that carries out the DNA's instruction. Life continues normally until the DNA ceases to form the RNA after which cell regeneration is seriously inhibited or stopped. When this becomes widespread, death is the final result.

In the 1977 issue of the **Journal of the International Academy of Preventative Medicine**, Dr. Ivan Popov gives two important reasons of supplementing the diet with raw glandular concentrates. They are:
1. Poor nutrition
2. Aging

That pretty much means all of us, as no one escapes aging, especially now when organ meats are rarely included in the diet, glandular nutrition affects almost everyone.

Raw glandulars include a wide variety:

adrenal
kidney
pituitary
thymus
stomach
thyroid
pancreas
duodenum
male testes and prostate
female ovaries and uterus
brain
heart
liver

If you feel that you are in need of a glandular, you should at least consider a multiglandular concentrate. Such a product contains tissue from all the principal glands and helps provide balanced nutrition for these important organs. Multiglandulars can be taken regularly with complete safety, just like supplemental vitamins and minerals. Your multi-glandulars are usually a low potency and will just support those important glands, not try to take them over such as drugs do in the body. When taking singular glandular concentrates, they shouldn't be taken on a regular basis for any longer than 9 to 12 weeks, as they have a tendency to take over the job the gland should be doing.

Tests conducted in both Europe and the U.S. indicate that freeze-drying yields the most biological active raw gland concentrates. Freeze-drying preserves all gland functions. Raw glandulars should be made only from animals that have been grazed solely on clean range land. Look for freeze-dried concentrates from imported livestock. Remember - you are only as old as your glands, nourish those important organs well and you will enjoy the youthful glow of good health for years and years to come. The key concept in glandular therapy is that like cells help like cells.

Appendix

TABLE 1*
Some Nutrients Dependent on Each Other

*Supplied through the courtesy of the Nutrionics Literature Search, 624 N. Victory Blvd., Burbank, CA 91502 (213) 841-7200.

Nutrient	Complementary Nutrients	Anti-Vitamins	Bodily Functions Affected	Deficiency Symptoms
Vitamin A Fat soluble	B complex, choline, C, D, E, F, calcium, zinc	alcohol, coffee, cortisone, excessive iron, mineral oil, vitamin D deficiency	body tissue reparation and maintenance (resist infection). Visual purple production (necessary for night vision.)	allergies, appetite loss, blemishes, dry hair, fatigue, itching burning eyes, loss of smell, night blindness, rough dry skin, sinus trouble, soft tooth enamel, susceptibility to infections
Vitamin B₁ Water soluble	B complex, B₂, folic acid, niacin, C, E, manganese, sulphur	alcohol, coffee, fever, raw clams, sugar (excess), stress, surgery, tobacco	appetite, blood building, carbohydrate metabolism, circulation, digestion (hydrocholoric acid production), energy, growth, learning capacity, muscle tone maintenance (intestines, stomach, heart)	appetite loss, digestive disturbances, fatigue, irritability, nervousness, numbness of hands & feet, pain & noise sensitivity, pains around heart, shortness of breath

107

TABLE 1 Continued

Nutrient	Complementary Nutrients	Anti-Vitamins	Bodily Functions Affected	Deficiency Symptoms
Vitamin B₂ Water soluble	B complex, B₆, niacin, C, phosphorus	alcohol, coffee, sugar (excess), tobacco	antibody & red blood cell formation, cell respiration, metabolism (carbohydrate, fat, protein)	cataracts, corner of mouth cracks & sores, dizziness, itching burning eyes, poor digestion, retarded growth, red sore tongue
Vitamin B₆ Water soluble	B complex, B₁, B₂, pantothenic acid, C, magnesium, potassium, linoleic acid, sodium	alcohol, birth control pills, coffee, radiation (exposure), tobacco	antibody formation, digestion (hydrochloric acid production), fat & protein utilization (weight control), maintains sodium potassium balance (nerves)	acne, anemia, arthritis, convulsions in babies, depression, dizziness, hair loss, irritability, learning disabilities, weakness
Vitamin B₁₂, Water soluble	B complex, B₆, choline, inositol, C, potassium, sodium	alcohol, coffee, laxatives, tobacco	appetite, blood cell formation, cell longevity, healthy nervous system, metabolism (carbohydrate, fat, protein)	general weakness, nervousness, pernicious anemia, walking and speaking difficulties

Nutrient	Complementary Nutrients	Anti-Vitamins	Bodily Functions Affected	Deficiency Symptoms
Biotin, B complex Water Soluble	B complex, B_{12}, folic acid, pantothenic acid, C, sulphur	alcohol, coffee, raw egg white (avidin)	cell growth, fatty acid production, metabolism (carbohydrate, fat, protein), vitamin B utilization	
Vitamin C Water Soluble	all vitamins & minerals, bioflavonoids, calcium, magnesium	antibiotics, aspirin, cortisone, high fever, stress, tobacco	bone & tooth formation, collagen production, digestion, iodine conservation, healing (burns & wounds), red blood cell formation (hemorrhaging prevention), shock & infection resistance (colds), vitamin protection (oxidation)	anemia, bleeding gums, capillary wall ruptures, bruise easily, dental cavities, low infection resistance (colds), nose bleeds, poor digestion
Vitamin D Fat Soluble	A, choline, C, F, calcium, phosphorus	mineral oil	calcium & phosphorus metabolism (bone formation), heart action, nervous system maintenance, normal blood clotting, skin respiration	burning sensation (mouth & throat), diarrhea, insomnia, myopia, nervousness, poor metabolism, softening bones & teeth

TABLE 1 Continued

Nutrient	Complementary Nutrients	Anti-Vitamins	Bodily Functions Affected	Deficiency Symptoms
Vitamin E Fat Soluble	A, B complex, B₁, inositol, C, F, manganese, selenium, phosphorus	birth control pills, chlorine, mineral oil, rancid fat & oil	aging retardation, anti-clotting factor, blood cholesterol reduction, blood flow to heart, capillary wall strengthening, fertility, male potency, lung protection (anti-pollution), muscle and nerve maintenance	dry, dull, or falling hair; enlarged prostate gland; gastrointestinal disease; heart disease; impotency; miscarriages; muscular wasting; sterility
Vitamin F Unsaturated fatty acids	A, C, D, E, phosphorus	radiation, x-rays	artery hardening prevention, blood coagulation, blood pressure normalizer, cholesterol destroyer, glandular activity, growth, vital organ respiration	acne, allergies, diarrhea, dry skin, dry brittle hair, eczema, gallstones, nail problems, underweight, varicose veins
Vitamin P Bioflavonoids	vitamin C	same as vitamin C	blood vessel wall maintenance, bruising minimization, cold & flu prevention, strong capillary maintenance	same as C (especially tendency to bleed & bruise easily)

Nutrient	Complementary Nutrients	Anti-Vitamins	Bodily Functions Affected	Deficiency Symptoms
Choline Water Soluble	A, B complex, B₁₂, folic acid, inositol, linoleic acid	alcohol, coffee, sugar (excessive)	lecithin formation, liver & gallbladder regulation, metabolism (fats, cholesterol), nerve transmission	bleeding stomach ulcers, growth problems, heart trouble, high blood pressure, impaired liver & kidney functions, intolerance to fats
Folic Acid Water Soluble	B complex, B₁₂, biotin, pantothenic acid, C	alcohol, coffee, stress, tobacco	appetite, body growth & reproduction, hydrochloric acid production, protein, metabolism, red blood cell formation	anemia, digestive disturbances, graying hair, growth problems
Inositol	B complex, B₁₂, B₂, C, Phosphorus	alcohol, coffee	artery hardening retardation, cholesterol reduction, hair growth, lecithin formation, metabolism (fat & cholesterol)	cholesterol (high), constipation, eczema, eye abnormalities, hair loss

TABLE 1 Continued

Nutrient	Complementary Nutrients	Anti-Vitamins	Bodily Functions Affected	Deficiency Symptoms
Niacin Water Soluble	B complex, B_1, B_2, C, phosphorus	alcohol, antibiotics, coffee, corn, sugar, starches (excessive)	circulation, cholesterol level reduction, growth, hydrochloric acid production, metabolism (protein, fat, carbohydrate), sex hormone production	appetite loss, canker sores, depression, fatigue, halitosis, headaches, indigestion, insomnia, muscular weakness, nausea, nervous disorders, skin eruptions
Pantothenic Acid Water Soluble	B complex, B_6, B_{12}, biotin, folic acid, C	alcohol, coffee	antibody formation, carbohydrate, fat, protein conversion (energy), growth stimulation, vitamin utilization	diarrhea, duodenal ulcers, eczema, hypoglycemia, intestinal disorders, kidney trouble, loss of hair, muscle cramps, premature aging, respiratory infections, restlessness, nerve problems, sore feet, vomiting
PABA, Para Amino-benzoic Acid B complex	B complex, folic acid, C	alcohol, coffee, sulfa drugs	blood cell formation, graying hair (color restoration), intestinal bacteria activity, protein metabolism	constipation, depression, digestive disorders, fatigue, gray hair, headaches, irritability

112

Nutrient	Complementary Nutrients	Anti-Vitamins	Bodily Functions Affected	Deficiency Symptoms
Calcium	A, C, D, F, iron, magnesium, manganese, phosphorus	lack of exercise, stress (excessive)	bone & tooth formation, blood clotting, heart rhythm, nerve tranquilization, nerve transmission, muscle growth & contraction	heart palpitations, insomnia, muscle cramps, nervousness, arm & leg numbness, tooth decay
Chromium	none	none	blood sugar level, glucose metabolism (energy)	atherosclerosis, glucose intolerance in diabetics
Copper	cobalt, iron, zinc	zinc (high intakes)	bone formation, hair & skin color, healing processes of body, hemoglobin & red blood cell formation	general weakness, impaired respiration, skin sores
Iodine	none	none	energy production, metabolism (excess fat), physical & mental development	cold hands & feet, dry hair, irritability, nervousness, obesity

TABLE 1 Continued

Nutrient	Complementary Nutrients	Anti-Vitamins	Bodily Functions Affected	Deficiency Symptoms
Iron	B₁₂, folic acid, C, calcium, cobalt, copper, phosphorus	coffee, excess phosphorus, tea, zinc (excessive intake)	hemoglobin production, stress & disease resistance	breathing difficulties, brittle nails, iron deficiency anemia (pale skin, fatigue), constipation
Magnesium	B₆, C, D, calcium, phosphorus	none	acid alkaline balance, blood sugar metabolsim (energy), metabolism (calcium & vitamin C)	confusion, disorientation, easily aroused anger, nervousness, rapid pulse, tremors
Manganese	none	calcium, phosphorus (excessive intake)	enzyme activation, reproduction & growth, sex hormone production, tissue respiration, vitamin B₁ metabolism, vitamin E utilization	ataxia (muscle coordination failure), dizziness, ear noises, loss of hearing

Nutrient	Complementary Nutrients	Anti-Vitamins	Bodily Functions Affected	Deficiency Symptoms
Potassium	B_6, sodium	alcohol, coffee, cortisone, diuretics, laxatives, salt (excess), sugar (excess), stress	heartbeat, rapid growth, muscle contraction, nerve tranquilization	acne, continuous thirst, dry skin, constipation, general weakness, insomnia, muscle damage, nervousness, slow irregular heartbeat, weak reflexes

Table 2
Recommended Optimum Personal Allowances (OPAs) for Vitamins

	Weight (±20 lbs.)	Height (±5")	Vita-min A (IU)	Vita-min D (IU)	Vita-min E (IU)	Vita-min C (mg)	Folic Acid (mcg)	Thia-min B₁ (mg)	Ribo-flavin B₂ (mg)	Nia-cin B₃ (mg)	Vita-min B₆ (mg)	Vita-min B₁₂ (mcg)	Bio-tin (mcg)	Panto-thenic Acid (mg)	Inos-itol (mg)	PABA (mg)	Pan-gam-ate (mg)	Bio-flavo-noids (mg)
MALES																		
Age: 19-35	147	69																
Lower limit			5,000	400	100	1,000	500	50	50	100	50	50	50	100	100	50	25	50
Upper limit			10,000	600	200	2,000	1,000	150	150	300	150	150	150	200	200	150	75	100
Age: 36-50	154	69																
Lower limit			5,000	400	200	1,000	500	100	100	100	100	100	100	100	100	100	25	50
Upper limit			10,000	600	400	3,000	1,000	150	150	300	200	150	150	200	200	150	75	100
Age: 51+	154	69																
Lower limit			10,000	400	400	2,000	500	100	100	200	100	100	100	100	100	100	25	50
Upper limit			15,000	600	600	4,000	1,000	200	200	400	200	200	200	300	300	200	50	100
FEMALES																		
Age: 19-35	128	65																
Lower limit			5,000	400	100	1,000	500	50	50	100	100	50	50	100	100	50	25	50
Upper limit			10,000	600	200	2,000	1,000	150	150	300	200	150	150	200	200	150	75	100
Age: 36-50	128	65																
Lower limit			7,000	400	100	1,000	500	100	100	100	200	100	100	100	100	100	25	50
Upper limit			12,000	600	300	3,000	1,000	150	150	300	300	150	150	200	200	150	75	100
Age: 51+	128	65																
Lower limit			10,000	600	400	2,000	500	100	100	200	100	100	100	100	100	100	25	50
Upper limit			15,000	800	600	4,000	1,000	200	200	400	200	200	200	300	300	200	50	100

NOTE: IU = International Units; mg = milligrams; mcg = micrograms.

ANALGESIA IN HUMAN PAIN PATIENTS IN RESPONSE TO D-PHENYLALANINE

Condition	Duration	Prior Treatment	Time on DPA	Result
Whiplash	2 years	Empirin, Valium	3 days	Complete relief, 1 month
Osteoarthritis, fingers, thumbs of both hands	5 years	Empirin, aspirin	maintained	Excellent relief; joint stiffness reduced
Rheumatoid arthritis (left knee), oesteoarthritis of hands	several years	Empirin + codeine	1 week	Considerable relief
Low back pain, neck pain	several years	90 acupunctures	3 days	Low back pain gone; walked one mile
Low back pain	several years	Spinal fusion, percutaneous nerve stimulation	3 days	Much less pain
Low back pain	several years	Laminectomies, Depomedrol, percutaneous nerve stimulation	3 days	Good to excellent relief
Fibrositis of muscle	?	Empirin	3 days	Pain gone, recurred after 2 days
Migraine headache	several years		2 days	Good relief, may prevent recurrence
Cervical osteoarthritis plus postoperative pain	?	?	2 days	Very little pain
Severe lower back pain	several years	Empirin, Valium	3 days	Excellent relief

Table 3

ALZHEIMER'S DISEASE

* Oral chelation

Completely eliminate the use of all aluminum cooking utensils and aluminum drinking utensils.

Stop the use of aluminum foil, especially in baking as there is a transfer of aluminum to the food through heat. Even the use of aluminum foil when baking a fowl or roast also allows the transfer of aluminum through heat -- *this also includes baked potatoes and pies!* The use of a Muscle Response Test will quickly show the fallacy of using aluminum foil in cooking.

Exercise regularly.

Use glandulars to restore the RNA and the DNA factor *(refer to the section of glandulars)*, and multiple glandulars would probably be best. Do not use antiperspirant deodorants as they contain aluminum chlorohydrates. Also commercial baking powder contains aluminum.

* Oral chelation is a method of taking orally into the body those substances that will break down and help to remove such detrimental things as calcium, lead, mercury, aluminum, and other substances that cause harm to the brain and can cause hardening of the arteries (arteriosclerosis). You are only as healthy as your circulatory system in that its job is to provide every cell in the body with adequate amounts of nutrition, and when it slows down, the cells begin to starve and then we become candidates for strokes and heart attacks. The A.M.A. feels the only answer is By-pass surgery--we feel there are others.

CANDIDA ALBICANS

Candida Albicans is a friendly bacteria in the bowel. As long as it is in the bowel, there is no problem. It is when it causes fungus infection outside of the bowel that problems begin to show up.

Candida Albicans can cause thrush and vaginal infections. It can, in fact, mimic almost any disease from eye infection to allergy to colitis, cystitis, gastritis, brain tumor, multiple sclerosis, and even insanity. There are even more symptoms: depression; lethargy; agitation; loss of memory and concentration; headaches; dizziness; insomnia; disturbance in smell, taste, vision, hearing; sensitivity to chemical odors, fragrances, foods; weight loss or gain; hay fever; bronchitis; hives, menstrual irregularities; bloating; diarrhea or constipation; Chrohn's disease; arthritis; myasthenia gravis; vaginal yeast infections; and prostatitis. It is also believed that the majority of all prostatitis is Candida Albicans.

Major problems come from the use of Cortisone, birth control pills, and antibiotics. Many allergies are caused by the hidden candida fungi. People who have developed susceptibility to this problem must follow a very strict diet in order to bring the ever present Candida under control. Certainly improving the immune system and restoring it to its natural state is the best advice that can be given.

The medical profession uses a drug called Nystatin--it is an anti-fungi drug. There are also many herbs that are anti-fungal.

Candida is often misdiagnosed. Another one is Premenstrual Syndrome. Candida Albicans and Premenstrual Syndrome go together like twin sisters. Symptoms of the two conditions are quite similar and should be treated concurrently for a complete cure. Premenstrual Syndrome, they have found, is majorly involved with the pituitary and thyroid glands, which influence the hormone balance in women.

The use of acidophilus is a must as it is one thing that will contain and control the Candida in the colon. It has been through the loss of the acidophilus bacteria that the Candida was allowed to escape from the bowel, causing its problems.

There are many things that will destroy the acidophilus in the colon such as red meat, which is generally high in antibiotics that are given to the animal in order to guarantee that it will make its way to the slaughterhouse. Coffee also destroys the acidophilus bacteria.

Although we need to stay away from milk products, acidophilus (though made from milk) is not a problem. Generally 10 fifty-million acidophilus capsules twice a day will get the job done if used for approximately three months. The person is sometimes a year to two years bringing the Candida completely under control and destroying it at the cellular level. (Refer to p. 34 for more information on Acidophilus.)

DIETARY SUPPRESSION OF CANDIDA ALBICANS

A. The yeast grows on sugar and starch and is fed by gluten-containing grains. Gluten grains include wheat, oats, rye, and barley.

  1. Do not eat sugar or sweets. **This includes** products made with honey or molasses as well as sugar.

  2. Do not eat wheat, oats, rye, or barley. Corn, rice, potatoes, buckwheat, and millet may be eaten in very small quantities by most individuals. *Some people, however, must temporarily exclude all of these starchy foods from the diet.*

  3. Milk (even raw) encourages Candida growth. Avoid milk and milk products except butter.

B. Yeast, molds, and fungi cross-react. When taken in food or even breathed in high concentrations, they trigger symptoms and diminish the body's resistance to Candida. Bathrooms and air vents should be kept clean and dry. Yeast, mold and fungus should be minimized in foods.

  1. Yeast is used in food preparation and flavoring:

    (a) Commercial breads, rolls, coffee cakes, pastries, etc.

    (b) Beer, wine, and all alcoholic beverages.

    (c) Most commerical soups, barbecue potato chips, and dry roasted nuts.

    (d) Vinegar and vinegar-containing foods such as pickled vegetables, sauerkraut, relishes, green olives, and salad dressing. Lemon juice with oil may be used as a salad dressing.

    (e) Soy sauce, cider and natural root beer.

2. Yeast is the basis for many vitamin and mineral preparations. Tryptophan is often derived from yeast.

3. Molds build up on foods while drying, smoking, curing and fermenting.

   (a) Avoid pickled, smoked, or dried meats, fish, and poultry, including sausages, salami, hot dogs, pickled tongue, corned beef, pastrami, smoked sardines and other fish that have been dried or smoked.

   (b) Bacon should be avoided. Country-style cured pork, of all kinds is loaded with mold.

   (c) Dried fruits such as prunes, raisins, dates, figs, citrus peels, candied cherries, currants, peaches, apples, and apricots should be avoided.

   (d) All cheeses (including cottage cheese), sour cream, buttermilk, and milk should be avoided.

   (e) Chocolate, honey, maple syrup and nuts accumulate mold and should not be eaten.

4. Melons (expecially cantaloupe) and the skins of fleshy vegetables or fruits accumulate mold during growth.

5. Avoid canned or frozen citrus, grape, and tomato juice. Avoid all canned or frozen foods which contain citric acid.

6. Mushrooms are fungi. Do note eat them.

7. Drinking coffee destroys Acidophilus in the colon, releasing the Candida and enabling it to get into the bloodstream.

C. Eating fruit will boost blood sugar levels and encourage yeast growth. Fruits and fruit juices must be temporarily omitted from the diet.

D. Teas, including herb teas, and spices are dried foods and accumulate molds. Avoid some herb teas and dried spices.

E. We need to emphasize that any vitamin supplements taken should be yeast-free until the Candida is under control, then you can return to your normal supplements with yeast in them. 123

What is Left to Eat?

PROTEINS:

Fish, chicken, turkey, duck, seafood, eggs, pheasant, quail, lamb, veal. In other words, animals if the meat is fresh instead of dried, smoked, pickled, or cured.

VEGETABLES:

All vegetables are potentially acceptable. Only starchy ones such as potatoes and sweet potatoes must be avoided by some people.

Is it Possible to Eat Out?

Yes! *Just order carefully.* Skip the cocktail. Have oil and lemon juice on your salad. Order meat, chicken, or other animal protein that is prepared without sauces which might contain *sugar, mushrooms, wheat as a thickener, and other harmful ingredients. Broiled or plain items are obviously the safest choice. Steamed vegetables are perfect!* **Skip bread, crackers, and dessert.**

The use of such herbs as Garlic, Red Raspberry, Pau D'Arco, Sarsaparilla, Sage, White Oak Bark, and Black Walnut are all recommended as they are antifungal herbs (*refer to **The Little Herb Encyclopedia, Revised** for more information on these herbs*). Certainly the use of Vitamin A, which is the antibiotic vitamin, will enhance the immune system--that along with Vitamin C. Some physicians are recommending as high as 200,000 i.u.'s of Vitamin A a day. The use of acidophilus is a *must!*.

One good naturopathic physician has found that we should be on a diet not to exceed 80 grams of carbohydrates a day.

124

MULTIPLE SCLEROSIS AND ALS

AVOID:

Eggs
Wheat
Rye-Oats
Chocolate
Spinach
Mild
Sodas
Cocoa
Coffee
Nuts
Strawberries
Dry Fruits
Prune Juice
Pork
Fish
Red meat
Shell fish
Cheese

Fried Foods
Corn
Cucumber
Onions
Radishes
Tomatoes
Olives
Peanut Butter
Pickles
Relishes
Spices
Tobacco Smoking
Gluten
Yeast
Bananas
Avocados
Novacaine

USE:

B-Complex (yeast-free)
B12 (yeast-free)
Vitamin E
Vitamin C
Lecithin
Calcium & Magnesium
Substituted Polyunsaturates
Fats for saturated ones
*Evening Primrose Oil
Multiple Male Glandular or Multiple Female Glandular
Cod Liver Oil - 5 grams
Vegetable Oil - 10-15 grams
Oral Chelation
Mineral Maintenance
Vitamin A & D
Histamine
Curane
Exercise - Energizer
Reverse Osmosis (R.O.) Water
*Scullcap
*Combination 8
*HVS
*RE-X

References:

Dr. Boines
Delare Med. Journal Vol. 40
#2 February, 1968, p. 34

Dr. Jonez

*Refer to *The Little Herb Encyclopedia, Revised* by this author for further information on these herbs.

PREMENSTRUAL SYNDROME (PMS)

Premenstrual Syndrome has just rencently come to light as it was passed off for many years by the medical profession who claimed it was just women wanting attention when in actuality it is a body completely out of balance screaming for help. (Refer to Candida Albicans).

The use of a mutliple glandular would be very beneficial. Also the need for Vitamin E is a must. Such herbs as Black Cohosh and Dong Quai need to be considered. Female corrective herbal formulas such as FCS II, FC with Dong Quai, and NF-X need to be considered. Refer to *The Little Herb Encyclopedia, Revised* for further information on the use of herbs in this condition.

Bibliography

Adams, Ruth. *The Complete Home Guide to All the Vitamins.*
New York: Larchmont Books, 1972.

Adams, Ruth, and Murray, Frank. *Minerals: Kill or Cure.*
New York: Larchmont Books, 1976.

Battista, Al, *"Candida Albicans"*

Bieri, John G. "Fat-soluble vitamins in the eighth revision of
the Recommended Dietary Allowances." *Journal of the
American Dietetic Association 64* (February 1974).

Borsaak, Henry. *Vitamins: What They Are and How They
Can Benefit You.* New York: Pyramid Books, 1971.

"Candida Albicans." Maureen Salaman Interviews Al Battista,
N.D., *Health Express,* November, 1984.

Ebon, Martin. *Which Vitamins Do You Need?* New York:
Bantam Books, 1974.

Goodhart, Robert S., and Shills, Maurice E. *Modern
Nutrition in Health and Disease.* 5th ed. Philadelphia: Lea
and Febiger, 1973.

Griffin, LaDean. *Please Doctor, I'd Rather Do It Myself...
with Vitamins & Minerals.* Salt Lake City: Hawkes
Publishing, Inc., 1979.

Katz, Marcella. *Vitamins, Food, and Your Health.* Public
Affairs Committee, 1971, 1975.

Martin, Marvin. *Great Vitamin Mystery.* Rosemont, IL:
National Dairy Council, 1978.

McGraw-Hill Book Co. New York City, *Nutritional Almanac.*
1979.

Mindell, Earl. *Earl Mindell's Vitamin Bible.* New York:
Rawson, Wade Publishers, Inc., 1980.

Null, Gary and Steve. *The Complete Book of Nutrition.* New
York: Dell, 1972.

Rodale, J.I. The Complete Book of Minerals for Health. 4th
ed. Emmaus, PA: Rodale Books, 1976.

Rosenberg, Harold, and Feldzaman, A.N. *Doctor's Book of
Vitamin Therapy: Megavitamins for Health.* New York:
Putnam's, 1974.

"Vitamin-Mineral Safety, Toxicity and Misuse." *Journal of the
American Dietetic Association,* 1978.

Wade, Carlson. *Magic Minerals.* West Nyack, NY: Parker
Publishing Co., 1967.

Additional Books Written by Dr. Jack Ritchason and Verlyn Ritchason

Cook Right to Eat Right
by Verlyn Ritchason, B.S., N.C.
This attractive cookbook brings a bit of nature's sunshine to your kitchen table—with recipes so good you'll think Mother Nature made them!
Spiral bound

The Little Herb Encyclopedia, Revised
by Dr. Jack Ritchason, N.D., Ph.D.
No longer is exclusive research necessary before using Nature's medicine - this is a ready reference, a quick way to find answers to your most common herb questions.
126 pages, quality paperback

HOME-STUDY COURSE IN IRIDOLOGY

By Dr. Jack Ritchason, N.D., R.H., T.H.I., I.D., Ph.D.
and Verlyn Ritchason, B.S., N.C.

Opthalmo-Analysis (the study of the Iris, Pupil and Sclera)
Part I - Iridology Home Study Course

Write for Information on advanced course
in Iridology!

Write To:
Jack Ritchason, N.D., Ph.D.
2425 Haley St.
Bakersfield, Calif. 93305